THE CHILDREN OF SOLAGA

The Children of Solaga

Indigenous Belonging across the U.S.-Mexico Border

DAINA SANCHEZ

STANFORD UNIVERSITY PRESS
Stanford, California

Stanford University Press
Stanford, California

Printed in the United States of America on acid-free, archival-quality paper.

Library of Congress Cataloging-in-Publication Data

Names: Sanchez, Daina, author.
Title: The children of Solaga : indigenous belonging across the U.S.-Mexico border / Daina Sanchez.
Description: Stanford, California : Stanford University Press, [2025] | Includes bibliographical references and index.
Identifiers: LCCN 2024012337 (print) | LCCN 2024012338 (ebook) | ISBN 9781503640221 (cloth) | ISBN 9781503641372 (paperback) | ISBN 9781503641389 (ebook)
Subjects: LCSH: Indians of Mexico—California—Los Angeles—Ethnic identity. | Indians of Mexico—California—Los Angeles—Social life and customs. | Indians of Mexico—Mexico—Oaxaca (State)—Social life and customs. | Mexicans—California—Los Angeles—Social life and customs. | Immigrants—Cultural assimilation—California—Los Angeles. | San Andrés Solaga (Mexico)—Social life and customs.
Classification: LCC F869.L89 M568 2025 (print) | LCC F869.L89 (ebook) | DDC 972/.7400497–dc23/eng/20240808
LC record available at https://lccn.loc.gov/2024012337
LC ebook record available at https://lccn.loc.gov/2024012338

Cover design: Lindy Kasler
Cover photograph: Irvine Carrillo
Typeset by Newgen in 11/15 Arno Pro

Para da Din Cansec y Elica Pio

CONTENTS

ACKNOWLEDGMENTS

I am the daughter, granddaughter, great-granddaughter, and the descendant of displaced peoples. And yet, I have never felt out of place. I am first and foremost grateful to my mother and my grandmother who always made sure I knew who I was and where I came from. They ensured I became a proud Solagueña and a proud descendant of Yojoveños and Yatenses. I am even more proud, however, to be their daughter and granddaughter. My life and this book would not be the same if I were not blessed with the women who instilled in me the love and appreciation for our community and our way of life that served as the inspiration for this book.

I am forever grateful for my family whose love, encouragement, and reminders that *querer es poder* continue to motivate me. As a child, my father dreamed of the day he would be able to read the papers he came across on his way home from school. He instilled in me his thirst for knowledge and his love for reading; I wish he were here to read all of the pages his daughter wrote. I give thanks to my sisters Shaina, Enedina, and Francisca, the funniest people I know, for bringing even more joy and laughter to my life. I am excited to spend more time with you now that the book is finished.

A million thanks to my family in Oaxaca who helped make this transnational endeavor possible, especially Jaquelina Arce and Jairo Arce. I sincerely thank Hidalia, Israel, Lizbeth, and Francisco Sánchez for welcoming me into their home in Santo Domingo Yojovi. I am deeply appreciative of Carolina Martínez, Alberta Julian, and Elizabeth Vicente for their friendship and medicine and for entertaining my attempts to speak Yojovi Zapotec. They might not realize it, but it means the world to me that they help me connect with my great-grandmother's language. I thank my *angelitos* Bonifacio, Margarita, Leonides, and Juan Arce. As my mother likes to remind me, they are always looking out for me.

To Andrea Cruz, thank you for hyping the book every step of the way. To Irvine Carrillo, who took the photograph that became the book cover, it means so much to me to see you develop your many talents across the years. My sincere gratitude to Leonel Arce for the childhood memories *y por los jarabes que nos falta echarnos.*

I am forever indebted to *Banda Juvenil Solaga USA Oaxaca* and their parents for allowing me to conduct research with them and generously offering their time and insight. I am also indebted to the municipal authorities of San Andrés Solaga for allowing me to conduct research in the community. This research would not be possible without *paisanos* across generations and borders who helped me articulate many of the things I would never have been able to name on my own. I thank them for opening their homes and sharing their stories with me. To the *wekuell* and *weya'* past, present, and future, may our lives be forever filled with the joy your music and dance inspire.

I would like to express my appreciation to the mentors and friends I have made during my academic journey. I thank Dr. Michelle Madsen Camacho, who opened my eyes to the world of research and who has offered her guidance throughout this journey. Leo R. Chavez's generosity, guidance, and mentorship saw this research project and book into fruition. As did the support of Susan B. Coutin, Raúl Fernandez, Laura E. Enriquez, and Rubén G. Rumbaut during my time at the University of California, Irvine. I would like to extend my gratitude to Keisha-Khan Y. Perry for providing me with the language to better articulate my community's experiences and to Paja Faudree, Jessaca Leinaweaver, Almita Miranda, and Irma Alicia Velásquez Nimatuj for their support during my time at Brown University. My sincere thanks to Luis Urrieta Jr., Rosa Urrieta, Blanca Azucena Pacheco, and Pablo Montes, whom I had the honor of meeting and sharing space with at the University of Texas at Austin. I am grateful for the support of my colleagues at the University of California, Santa Barbara, including Gerardo Aldana, Ralph Armbruster-Sandoval, Monika Banach, Giovanni

Batz, Sarah Rosalena Brady, D. Inés Casillas, Nadège T. Clitandre, Micaela Díaz-Sánchez, Joann Erving, Michael Demarte, Diane C. Fujino, San Juanita García, Charles R. Hale, Amy Gonzales, Celia Herrera-Rodriguez, Aída Hurtado, Fallon Leung, Alan Mojarro Franco, Margaret McMurtrey, Taylor M. Moore, Jessica López-Espino, Raquel Pacheco, Silvia Rodriguez-Vega, Chela Sandoval, Emiko Saldívar, Michael V. Singh, Paul Spickard, Barbara Endemaño Walker, France Winddance Twine, Terrance Wooten, and Bryan Zuniga.

My gratitude to my friends Justin Perez and Natali Valdez for showing me the ropes even as you were figuring it all out yourselves. To Leisy J. Abrego, Akhila L. Ananth, Floridalma Boj Lopez, Nathan Coben, Stephanie Corzo, Amy Chin, Yanet Lopez-Cardenas, Guilberly Louissaint, Mauricio Magaña, Analicia Mejia Mesinas, Michael Warren Murphy, Brenda Nicolas, Mark Ocegueda, Simone Popperl, M. Liliana Ramirez, Luis Sánchez-López, Wynona Peters, Linda E. Sanchez, Heather K. Thomas, and Gretel Vera-Rosas for their company, friendship, and support.

To the Oaxacan students I have had the honor to mentor during my time at UCSB: Rocio Curiel, Karen Gonzalez-Salazar, Itzel Gutierrez Maldonado, Abigail Morales, Nancy Morales, Juan de Dios Pacheco Marcial, Angeliza Sanchez, and Soledad Sosa-Fuentes, as well as the students in *El Colectivo de Pueblos Originarios* (CPOD), for their inspirational work. Processing the book cover with CPOD made all the early morning and late night writing sessions worth it.

Finally, a huge thank you to Dylan Kyung-lim White and Austin Michael Araujo at Stanford University Press for their guidance throughout the publication process and for supporting my vision for the book. I am grateful to the no-longer-anonymous reviewers for their thoughtful and generous feedback on the manuscript.

This research was supported by National Science Foundation Graduate Research Fellowship Program, a National Science Foundation Doctoral Dissertation Research Improvement Grant, and a Ford Foundation Postdoctoral Fellowship, as well as several internal grants from the University of California, Irvine, and the University of California, Santa Barbara.

THE CHILDREN OF SOLAGA

Introduction

THE IMAGE IS GRAINY, but I can make out the path that leads to my mother's childhood home. Around a dozen men holding musical instruments stand next to a water well waiting for my family and our guests to depart for the church. Some women hold a candle and a handful of gladiolas, while men carry large bundles of flowers and candles wrapped in brown paper. The municipal band and our guests start the procession from our family home to the Catholic church, and a five-minute walk turns into a twenty-minute endeavor due to the solemnity and magnitude of the event. The band walks by, slowly playing the music for a *canto* for *La Virgen del Carmen,* as the women sing:

> *Virgen del Carmen*
> *Virgen del Carmelo*
> *Ve ante mis ojos*
> *Y muerame luego*

As they come closer, I recognize people I have not seen in years: our next-door neighbor, my grandmother, and my mother's youngest brother. Then, finally, I see myself in a pink track suit holding my mother's hand. Her tight grasp both guides my 5-year-old self to the church and ensures that I do not fall as we navigate the mountainous terrain.

My mother comes into the garage remarking that she had been looking for me. I try to wipe away the tears as I contemplate how lively our family home was during the summer of 1995. "It's the right video, *comadre*," Domingo informs my mother in Zapotec. My mother stares at the screen. "There goes the deceased Rodrigo. They're all there. Look! My brother!" she exclaims as her older brother rushes past her 20-year-old self. "So many people that have passed away come out in this video, *comadre*," Domingo replies. "It's the right video," he concludes as he takes out the cassette from his VHS player. Domingo, a first-generation Solagueño immigrant[1] in his early sixties, hands my mother the video cassette, which is mislabeled *Fiestas Patrias 1995*. Domingo had called me into his garage during a family party in Los Angeles, California, to make sure the VHS tape he was going to lend us had footage of the *Virgen del Carmen* celebrations held in Solaga in 1995, the year my mother sponsored the festivities in honor of our community's major patron saints.

Thanks to Domingo and his extensive video collection of *fiestas*, I had just witnessed the first time I visited San Andrés Solaga, the Zapotec town in Oaxaca, Mexico, from which my parents migrated as teenagers in the mid-1980s. As a child, I did not understand the significance of this and the subsequent return trips I eventually made as an unaccompanied minor traveling under the care of flight attendants to participate in patron saint celebrations in my family's hometown. As an adult, I was flooded with a range of emotions: from sadness at seeing my now-deceased relatives so full of life, to fascination at reflecting upon myself as a child engaging in one of the transborder practices that would eventually serve as the basis for my research on the transborder lives and practices of the children of Indigenous immigrants. Thus, while an ethnography usually begins with an anecdote of the anthropologist entering the field, *The Children of Solaga* begins with my first experience of *home*.

Solagueños have been displaced from their Indigenous homeland for several generations. The Solagueño diaspora includes people living in Oaxaca City, Mexico City, and Los Angeles, California.[2] My parents and I are part of the Los Angeles–based Solagueño diaspora and belong to a transborder community that stretches from our hometown of Solaga to Los Angeles, where Solagueños began settling in the 1970s. Unlike Solagueños living in Mexican territory, the United States–Mexico border separates Los Angeles–based Solagueño immigrants—the majority of whom are in the country without authorization—from their homeland. Lynn Stephen suggests, "A transborder community is full of people accustomed to living in multiple localities and discontinuous social, economic, and cultural spaces."[3] Domingo's VHS collection demonstrates not only how Solagueños were already accustomed by the mid-1990s to living divided by the state-imposed borders that prevented many of them from returning to their hometown, but also how Solagueños circumvented these borders to remain connected to their homeland.

Fiesta videos comprise a larger set of practices that have allowed undocumented Solagueño immigrants to experience their hometown despite not being able to physically return. While it was becoming increasingly more difficult for people to enter the United States without authorization in the 1990s, globalization facilitated the circulation of videos and other objects. Still, Solagueños held onto the sensorial memories of their hometown and longed to experience what it *felt* like to be in Solaga during patron saint celebrations. The creation of *Banda Juvenil Solaga USA Oaxaca,* the first Los Angeles–based brass band composed solely of the children of Oaxacan immigrants, created a means through which diasporic Solagueños[4] could experience their hometown celebrations, as well as a space where they could model Indigenous practices of belonging rooted in their community's ways of knowing and being in the world for their children. The establishment of this youth band would transform how Solagueños and their children develop and maintain ties to their ancestral homeland.

The Children of Solaga examines how diasporic Indigenous children and youth form racial, ethnic, community, and national identities away from their ancestral homeland. This book examines the role of Indigenous practices of belonging, including participating in Oaxacan brass bands and *danzas* in the receiving community and embarking on return trips to the home community for patron saint celebrations, in processes of identity formation among diasporic Solagueño children and youth. A central question undergirding this work explores why the children of Indigenous immigrants, most of whom are born abroad, engage in these practices. Throughout the book, I consider how the racial, ethnic, legal, and cultural exclusion that Indigenous Latinx immigrants and their children experience in the United States influences their continued involvement and investment in their community of origin. Indeed, participating in Solagueño communal life allows children and youth to develop a sense of belonging to their Indigenous homeland as they are being ostracized because of their racial, ethnic, and national background in their new "homes" in the United States. Through their participation in communal life, diasporic Solagueño children and youth are initiated into *comunalidad,* an Indigenous way of knowing and being in the world through which individuals demonstrate community belonging and are inducted into *el goce comunal,* or the feeling of communal joy community members reap from their contributions to and participation in communal life.[5]

Bia chhelha yowiz

"Buenas tardes," I say as I walk by two men sitting in front of an adobe house.
Good afternoon.
"Buenas tardes," they reply.
"Bi che da Modest," one of them, an uncle, says to the other as I walk away.
The child of the deceased Modesto.
"Lebo bia chhelha yowiz?" the other man asks.
She's the one that comes back every year?
"Lebo," my uncle responds.
It's her.

This encounter is exemplary of my encounters with people living in Solaga. There, I am identified in several ways that are not my given name, but through my relational identities. To Solagueños, I am *bi che da Modest Yade'* or the child of the deceased Modesto of Yateé, *bi che Elica Pio* or Elica Arce's child, *bi xhesua da Pach Pio* or the grandchild of the deceased Bonifacio Arce, *bi xhesua da Din Cansec* or the grandchild of the deceased Enedina Canseco, and *bia chhelha yowiz* or the person that comes back every year.[6] *Bia chhelha yowiz* highlights my relationship to Solaga as a place and shows the importance Solagueño locals place on a transborder practice that I began as a 5-year-old child. Solagueños' usage of the word *chhelha* strikes me because it marks a sense of return. Embedded in this Zapotec verb is the idea that I return to the place in which I belong and from which I have been temporarily absent. If the verb were switched to *chhid,* Solagueño locals would be signaling a distance between not only Solaga and myself, but between them and myself. *Chhid* implies foreignness. An individual may come to Solaga but never really belong and thus they come but do not "come back" or "return."

I share how Solagueños see me in an effort to place myself in my field sites as a diasporic Solagueña turned researcher. This work breaks new ground as the first book-length ethnographic text written by a *nhol walhall*, or native woman from a community being studied: the children of Indigenous immigrants. *The Children of Solaga* tells the story of a people with shared origins in a particular place, growing up away from their ancestral homeland. In the Zapotec context, *bene walhall* translates to *paisanos* or local people. The adjective *walhall* places an emphasis on the humble origins of the object or person it describes.[7] While in the Western context humbleness or humility might have a negative connotation, Chicana feminists have long validated the experiences of poor, working-class peoples and found these worthy of being told and fruitful for the creation of new theory and methods.[8] Indigenous and Chicana feminists alike have rejected Western paradigms that posit that scholars must disassociate themselves from their lived experience in order to engage in knowledge production.[9] In writing this text from the subject position of a *nhol walhall*, I write and theorize from an emic understanding of social, ritual, and affective ties of a displaced Indigenous woman that, like her *bi walhall*, is oriented toward her ancestral homeland. *The Children of Solaga* thus interrupts anthropological traditions of studying Indigenous people as the static, "ethnographic other" and sees them as active agents, who can and do speak and theorize for and by themselves.[10]

My experiences as a researcher and as a second-generation Solagueña are not mutually exclusive. Like native anthropologists who share a common background with members of the societies they study, the children of Solagueños who visit their parents' hometown may have to grapple with societal norms and cultural taboos different from those of the United States. In Solaga, the children of Solagueño immigrants, myself included, discover they are not individuals, but extensions of their families. This construction of self and the family differs from the one we are accustomed to in the United States, where "youths are encouraged to be economically and socially independent to make decisions for themselves, and to believe that each individual is the best judge of what he or she wants and should do."[11]

In traveling to Solaga, American-reared youth must cope with a collective society where they are expected to comply with needs and values of the group for the sake of social cohesion.[12] As many visiting youth eventually find out, their actions in the town of Solaga become a reflection of their entire family. Thus, they are sometimes reprimanded for what might be considered bad behavior and at times encouraged to modify their behavior to maintain their family's good social standing, as discussed in Chapter 3. In some cases, as in other immigrant communities, differences in societal expectations could lead to conflict between visiting youth and Solagueño locals, jeopardizing the chances of satisfying and repeated return visits that could build an attachment and loyalty to their parents' hometown.[13]

My identity as *bia chhelha yowiz* also highlights various aspects of my privilege. As an American-born Solagueña, my U.S. citizenship allows me to move across the U.S.-Mexico border freely. Thus, I am able to "go back" every year. I do not take my U.S. citizenship for granted. Many first- and 1.5-generation[14] Solagueños are unable to travel to Solaga because of their legal status. As a student and now a university professor, I was and am still able to visit Solaga during the summer for the *Virgen del Carmen* celebration, the most important of my community's patron saint celebrations. Further, as a researcher, I have been able to secure funding to travel to Solaga, something that due to work and wage circumstances, many members of the community may be unable to do. Going back every year has also given me the social capital that allowed me to conduct this research. As the daughter of Solagueños residing in Los Angeles and a frequent visitor to Solaga, I was raised in Spanish- and Zapotec-speaking households on both sides of the United States–Mexico border and am a known member of the community. This background informs my worldview and the ways in which I interact with my interlocutors at my research sites, as well as the form this book takes.

In Solaga, the place I traveled to every summer since childhood, my presence was never questioned. Solagueños living in the home community have come to expect my presence during the summer months. During one of my first trips to Oaxaca during graduate school, a cousin asked me if I considered myself a tourist. Since we were in Oaxaca City at the time and he was taking me around because I was unfamiliar with the city, I answered, "Yes." He responded, "I don't consider you a tourist. You've come back every year since you were a little girl." It was then that I realized he was not asking if I considered myself a tourist in Oaxaca City, but in Solaga. Despite this misunderstanding, this conversation enlightened me on the way that at least one Solagueño regarded me. Even though I was not born in the community, I was not just another visitor. By virtue of traveling to Solaga every year, I belonged to and in the community in a particular way. This brought up questions for my own research. Are Solagueños who are unable to return to Solaga seen as less Solagueño? How do they navigate this? What happens to the children of immigrants who do return to Solaga but do not have good experiences, particularly children and youth whose artistry is integral to Solagueño community life in Los Angeles?

When I decided to conduct ethnographic research among Solagueños in Los Angeles, I approached *Banda Juvenil Solaga USA*, the Los Angeles–based Solagueño youth band, with the hope that they would allow me to conduct research with them. Since most band members were minors, this first meant getting approval from their parents. The parents who were part of the band's steering committee readily accepted. Some of the parents had known me since I was a child, while others simply knew of me. Although I engaged in return trips to Solaga throughout my childhood, my family did not frequent social gatherings and other celebrations in Los Angeles unless they were held by a close family member. We also did not attend these gatherings because when I was growing up, these celebrations were not held frequently. As I discuss in Chapter 2, the formation of the Solagueño youth band served as a catalyst for the Solagueño community, since band-organized fundraisers and patron saint celebrations gave Solagueño immigrants and their children a time and place to come together more regularly.

Since I neither frequented most of these events nor played in the band, the formation of my own identity as a diasporic Solagueña differs from the experience of my interlocutors who were involved in events in Los Angeles as dancers, musicians, and revelers. My positionality also meant that when I first began conducting research at these events in 2014, many people would express their surprise and joy that I was *conviviendo*, or socializing, with the community more frequently. Indeed, their remarks on the importance of *convivencia* with the community became integral to my understanding of Solagueño communal life in Los Angeles and Solaga, as I discuss in Chapter 3.

Throughout my time conducting fieldwork, I attended *Banda Juvenil Solaga USA*'s band practice sessions. I was close in age to some of the remaining original band members, but considerably older than the younger ones. This meant that while we spoke the same languages and grew up in the same community, there were still generational differences between us. Since many band members were minors and could not drive or did not have parents who could drive them to events, I volunteered to take them and their parents to their engagements, giving me more time to build rapport with them on the way to their performances. Many of the children of Solagueños I interviewed outside of the band were around the same age as me during the time I conducted fieldwork. Some I had met at family parties as a child. Others I met during return visits to Solaga. Still others I met during the course of fieldwork through family and friends. While speaking with the children of Solagueños, I realized the similarities and differences in our experiences and how these experiences have shaped our relationship with our parents' community across the U.S.-Mexico border. Our similarities included having parents from the town of Solaga who work at dry-cleaning businesses throughout the city of Los Angeles. Still, these similarities are shaped by other circumstances, including our parents' legal statuses, our own fluency in our parents' Indigenous language, and the neighborhoods in Los Angeles in which we were raised. For example, the ethnic composition of the neighborhoods in which we grew up determined the potential interactions between Solagueños and non-Indigenous Latinxs, which at times resulted in instances of discrimination, as I discuss in Chapter 2.

During the course of my fieldwork, I heard different ways that Solagueños across the U.S.-Mexico border imagine Solagueñoness. Some people saw being a Solagueño as merely having origins in the town of Solaga. Others saw it as participation in the community. Yet some believed that being a Solagueño meant one had to speak Zapotec, participate in *danzas,* or play in a band. I found that not partaking in these activities made some, particularly the children of immigrants, feel like they were not "as Solagueño" as their peers. Their point of reference was the children and youth in bands and dance groups in Los Angeles who have become the face of Oaxaca in Los Angeles. However, returning to Solaga may highlight differences in their lives in Los Angeles and the lives of people currently living in Solaga, as I discuss in Chapter 3. Like Takeyuki Tsuda, who conducted research among interlocutors who shared his origins in Japan, I often found that I was a sounding board for my informants as they reflected on their experiences as the children of immigrants in the sending and receiving community.[15] In the chapters that follow, I delve into the ways in which the children of immigrants are seen and see themselves. In addition to trans-border Solagueño community dynamics, settler-imposed racial hierarchies and systems of domination shape the ways in which diasporic children and youth identify and articulate their identities.

As the first book-length anthropological text on the children of Indige-nous immigrants written by a member of the community being studied, this work both breaks with and engages with anthropological convention. *The Children of Solaga* is influenced by my family histories, my experiences as a diasporic Solagueña, and traditional ethnographic methods. My relation-ship with my *pueblo* extends beyond my lifetime into relationships fostered by my ancestors alongside those of other Solagueños. My official period of ethnographic fieldwork, however, lasted from November 2014 through No-vember 2016. During this time, I conducted participant observation at three main sites: cultural group rehearsals in Los Angeles, patron saint festivi-ties and community events in Los Angeles, and patron saint celebrations in Solaga. I also interviewed first-generation Solagueño immigrants, 1.5- and second-generation Solagueños, and Solagueño locals. To protect the ano-nymity of my *paisanos*, I have changed names and identifying information.

Yell Zoolaga

San Andrés Solaga is a Zapotec community in the Sierra Norte region of Oaxaca.[16] The 2020 Mexican census enumerated 668 residents of Solaga.[17] This population may seem small in comparison to places like the city of Los Angeles, which is home to almost four million people.[18] Solaga remains a small town, yet lively when compared to neighboring "ghost villages," which are home to fewer than one hundred people as a result of periods of heavy emigration.[19] My mother likes to say that Solagueños are *gente que viene de todos lados*, or people who come from all over. This characterization of Solagueños contradicts ideas about Indigenous people, who are often thought of as stuck in place and time. Our community and my own family's history, however, challenges this narrative.

The ancestors of Solagueños migrated from the Valley of Oaxaca shortly before the Spanish invasion in the sixteenth century.[20] Solaga and the neighboring communities of Zoochogo and Tabaá were founded by three siblings who were originally from the Zapotec community of Zaachila. Our ancestors settled in Solaga's current location where they had found water and fertile land, which were lacking in the first two places they attempted to settle. Solaga received its name *zoolaga* (*zoo*: fallen or scattered, and *laga*: leaves) because of the leaves that fell from the trees in what became our home, the same leaves with which our ancestors built their homes. From its founding, Solaga has been a refuge for displaced peoples, including its first inhabitants and my ancestors.

My own ancestry reflects my mother's observation. To prove her point that *los Solagueños vienen de todos lados*, she reminds me that my paternal ancestors were not from Solaga but my father was born in the community and thus a Solagueño. Because of this, she assures me, I too am a Solagueña. On my mother's side, we can only trace our ancestry to Solaga. However, my father's grandfather and father were orphans from the neighboring Zapotec communities of San Francisco Yateé and Santo Domingo Yojovi. Because they were displaced by poverty and land conflict and orphaned at young ages, the only connections we have to these places are my father's Zapotec and Spanish surnames: *Yade'*, Sánchez, and Acevedo. My mother is right. My father and I are no longer considered Yojoveños or Yatenses despite our origins in those communities.[21] We became Solagueños. This is because to belong and to be recognized as members of Serrano communities, one must partake in communal life. As autonomous Indigenous communities, Yojovi and Yateé have the authority to determine community membership. As much as I consider people from Yojovi and Yateé my *paisanos*, I concede that I am not a Yojoveña or a Yatense. When I am in Yojovi, which is only a fifteen-minute drive from Solaga, I become hyperaware that I am and *feel* like a Solagueña. Yojoveños see me and I see myself as a Solagueña because of my sustained connection to Solaga and Solagueños. I am no longer connected to Yojovi or Yateé in the same way.[22] Some might ask how I and other diasporic Solagueños can claim membership to this

Indigenous community if belonging is premised on physical presence and active participation in the community. By virtue of living outside of our ancestral homeland, these connections should be severed. Nevertheless, diasporic Solagueños have adapted Indigenous practices of belonging to their lives in diaspora, allowing Solagueños and their children to maintain their connection to their homeland.[23]

There are approximately six hundred Solagueños residing in Los Angeles, California, including first-generation immigrants, their children, and grandchildren. We are part of an estimated two hundred fifty thousand Oaxacans living in Los Angeles.[24] In Los Angeles, it is rare for the children and grandchildren of Solagueños to speak Zapotec. I am one of a few Los Angeles-born Solagueños that can communicate in Zapotec beyond a few words or expressions. The 2020 Mexican census recorded that 80.99 percent of Solaga's population were Indigenous language speakers.[25] Some might say this makes these Solagueños "less Indigenous." However, in Solaga and in diaspora, language ideologies and processes of assimilation influence parental and individual decisions to learn or engage with Indigenous languages, as I discuss in Chapter 3. Accepting the Mexican state's criteria for determining Indigenous identity disregards state efforts to eradicate our languages and cultures and the reality that in Indigenous communities identity does not necessarily align with language ability.[26] *The Children of Solaga* instead focuses on the practices of belonging through which Solagueños determine and establish community membership, including through their participation in and enjoyment of *fiestas*. In doing so, diasporic Solagueños model how to build and maintain a relationship to their ancestral homeland for their children. Through community-based understandings of belonging, people who have come from many places and have had to migrate to many places have established and can still establish community membership in their ancestral homeland.

Diasporic Latinx Indigeneity

The Children of Solaga analyzes how diasporic Indigenous immigrants and their children continually remake their identities by looking at the cultural practices in honor of patron saints through which they maintain ties to their ancestral homeland. In doing so, this work contributes to (1) long-standing anthropological interests in Indigenous social organization and rituals, and (2) the interdisciplinary field of migration studies, particularly in the areas of Indigenous migration, immigrant adaptation and identity, and transnational migration. *The Children of Solaga* extends debates in migration studies and Indigenous studies by demonstrating that in addition to factors taken into account in studies of immigrant assimilation and incorporation in the United States—namely race, class, gender, and context of reception—settler colonial processes also influence how displaced Indigenous youth form their identities away from their community of origin. Indeed, U.S. settler ideologies construct White settlers as "natives" and privilege them and their descendants as the group most entitled to citizenship. Non-Whites in the U.S., in turn, exist within structures of racial and economic domination where their national belonging is constantly questioned. For the children of Indigenous immigrants who live between two settler states built on the elimination of Indigenous peoples, Indigenous practices of belonging become ways Indigenous immigrants and their children resist settler structures and policies that deny them the right to remain in their communities of origin and to create new communities in diaspora.

The Children of Solaga reckons with how diasporic Solagueño children and youth understand themselves as Indigenous peoples born or living outside of their homeland, as well as how non-Indigenous peoples respond to Solagueños' Indigenous background. Importantly, Indigenous people do not stop being Indigenous, become less Indigenous,[27] or stop being interpolated as Indigenous once they leave their homeland. In fact, many Latinxs uphold anti-Indigenous settler ideologies from Latin America that portray Indigenous peoples as inherently different and thus inferior to *mestizos*, who are people of mixed Indigenous and European ancestry. For peoples whose national identities are premised on ideologies of *mestizaje*, or racial mixing as a defining characteristic of cultural nationalism, Blackness and Indigeneity are relegated "to backwards moves within national imaginaries and nation-building projects that seek to move towards whiteness."[28] However, as Yomaira Figueroa-Vásquez points out with Afro-descendant peoples, diasporic peoples "are racialized in divergent ways, depending on their ethnic or national citizenship, location and ability to move or travel, class status, phenotype, and other factors."[29] In the Solagueño case, like their parents, diasporic Indigenous children and youth in Los Angeles are subjected to racial hierarchies instituted during and after colonization but most possess a settler-created status, American citizenship, which grants them privileges unavailable to their parents and ancestors. Still, as I demonstrate in Chapter 2, American citizenship does not guarantee their inclusion in American society.

Terms like "Indigenous" and "native" are relational and retrospective, since "natives" did not exist before their encounter with Europeans.[30] "Othering" Indigenous people allowed Europeans to justify expansion and colonization in the so-called New World. The discourse used to subjugate native peoples is similar to the tropes in American anti-immigrant discourse, which characterizes immigrants as "low class, subhuman, dangerous, foreign, morally inferior, and without history."[31] The similarities in anti-Indigenous and anti-immigrant tropes are not surprising, since the construction of the nation often relies on notions of inferiority and superiority. Fitzpatrick notes:

> The nation must also include what it excludes. It remains connected to the other. The other, in short, becomes the nation's double. There is a dual projection of identity onto this double. First, those characters which are contrary to the nation's positive, or posited, being are projected onto the double, with the nation taking on a coherent identity in opposition to them.[32]

The nation includes the "double," only to bolster national identity at the expense of the double. For the Mexican nation, unassimilated Indigenous peoples represent this double. Post-independence Mexican national identity relies on the myth of the *mestizo* nation, the product of the encounter between two great civilizations, the Spanish and the Aztec.[33] Non-*mestizos* were consequently deemed "a 'miscarriage' of the great prehispanic cultures."[34] The legacy of these negative attitudes toward Indigenous Mexicans manifests in the racism that Indigenous Mexican immigrants and their children continue to deal with at the hands of some *mestizo* immigrants in the United States.[35]

While most of the diasporic Solagueño youths I interviewed were born in the United States, their American citizenship did little to shield them from the impact their Indigenous origins had on their daily lives. As the children of Indigenous immigrants and Indigenous people themselves, youth were sometimes picked on at school and ridiculed for being "Oaxaquitas," a pejorative term used to describe Oaxacan-origin individuals with Indigenous physical features. Solagueño youth and other children of Indigenous immigrants may endure discrimination at the hands of *mestizo*-origin Latinxs as a result of their Indigenous language use, their lack of proficiency in English and Spanish, and their physical appearance.[36] In her work on undocumented Oaxacan youth, for example, Stephen has also found that Indigenous youth are racialized as inferior to their *mestizo* peers because of their cultural, linguistic, and geographic roots as Indigenous peoples.[37] As a result, Stephen argues, Indigenous cultural practices become instrumental for Indigenous immigrant youth to achieve some level of civic integration in their schools and community.

Still, others read diasporic Solagueño children and youth as "Mexicans" or Latinxs, identities that also carry negative connotations in the United States.[38] Diasporic Solagueño children and youth may be subject to xenophobia because of what Leo Chavez terms the Latino Threat Narrative. Proponents of this narrative assume all Mexicans, and by association all Latinxs, regardless of generation, are in the United States without authorization.[39] Through this narrative, not only are Latinxs portrayed as perpetual foreigners but their supposed "illegal" entry associates them with criminality, casting them as "illegal aliens."[40] Prejudice toward Solagueños on the basis of their national origin may stem from the suspicion that Mexicans are incapable or unwilling to integrate into American society.[41] The prevalence of the Latino Threat Narrative when applied to individuals who have been in the United States for several generations, however, demonstrates that racialized non-White individuals will likely always be considered foreign to the United States.

Indigenous Latinx immigrants and their children are uniquely positioned within U.S. and Latin American racial hierarchies. Solagueños' Indigeneity precludes them from being integrated into both the Mexican and American settler-states. In other words, while Solagueños may assimilate to Mexican and American ways of life by relinquishing aspects of their ethnic and national cultures, their racial background impedes them from being part of the national imaginary. In this way, the experiences of Solagueños are that of a diasporic people—the prejudices they endure are ongoing, structural, and interpersonal, even after endless sacrifices and attempts to merge into a new national community.[42] This difference, James Clifford argues, is what distinguishes diasporic people from immigrants who will eventually integrate into the national fold. Diasporic Solagueños may never be fully accepted as part of the national Mexican or American imaginary because of their ethnic, racial, and national background. In *The Children of Solaga*, however, I posit that the rejection diasporic Solagueños perceive from White Americans, Latinxs, and their co-nationals may drive their continued investment in their Indigenous identities and homeland.

Critical Latinx Indigeneities

Building on the Critical Latinx Indigeneities framework, *The Children of Solaga* understands Oaxacan cultural practices as a means through which Indigenous communities organize to ensure the survival of their collective identities while centering their ways of knowing and being in the world.[43] These practices are necessary as Indigenous immigrants and their children contend with displacement and migration from their places of origin, as well as state and police violence, economic exploitation, and racial discrimination.[44] Scholars working within the Critical Latinx Indigeneities framework urge academics and educators to familiarize themselves with the learning experiences of Indigenous Latinx youth as their families and cultural communities continue to instill in them "critical forms of Indigenous knowledges and cultural assets that contribute to the development, education, and well-being of Indigenous youth, their families and communities."[45] The knowledge and cultural assets Indigenous Latinx youth learn from their communities combine with their experiences in the U.S. to create new ways of being Indigenous.

Critical Latinx Indigeneities scholars have reflected on formative experiences that inform how they and their interlocutors understand identity and belonging as Indigenous peoples in diaspora.[46] Their work demonstrates how settler-imposed notions of Indigeneity and community-based understandings of belonging and identity inform millennial and emerging ways of organizing in community and redefine the types of community created in diaspora. A Critical Latinx Indigeneities framework allows scholars to explore the "creative forms of cultural cohesion" through which youth and Indigenous communities at large confront displacement and migration and ensure the survival of their distinct collectives[47] whether this be organizing around a *pueblo*[48] or an Indigenous ethnic identity.[49] *The Children of Solaga* employs the Critical Latinx Indigeneities framework to understand how Solagueño practices of belonging inform how diasporic Solagueños form their identities away from their homeland and how these practices mediate Indigenous displacement and marginalization.

Settler Colonialism

Central to the Critical Latinx Indigeneities framework and more recent scholarship on Indigenous Latin American migration to the United States is the recognition that colonial processes and racial hierarchies instituted by European settlers continue to affect the lives of Indigenous peoples throughout the Americas.[50] Put differently, Indigenous Mexican immigrants emigrate from one settler state with its own racial ideologies, Mexico, into another, the United States. Anglophone colonialism has been characterized as settler colonialism since Anglo settlers dispossessed Indigenous peoples from their land to expand their own economic enterprises and sociopolitical systems, created structures to eliminate and replace Indigenous cultures and knowledge, and cast themselves as the new "natives."[51] In places that undergo settler colonialism, Patrick Wolfe succinctly wrote, "The colonizers come to stay—invasion is a structure not an event."[52]

Settler colonialism has not been applied to a Latin American context, Shannon Speed argues, because colonialism in Latin America has been characterized by resource extraction and the marshaling of Indigenous labor. In her work on Indigenous women migrants from Mexico and Central America, Speed applies settler colonialism to Latin America, demonstrating how labor regimes in these territories facilitated Indigenous land dispossession and how the logic of elimination, a key pillar of settler colonialism, has manifested in Mexico and Central America through ideologies like *mestizaje*, an assimilationist project that promotes the racial mixing or cultural assimilation of Indigenous peoples as part of Latin American nation-building projects.[53] These nation-building projects propose that relinquishing Indigenous language and dress, along with other Indigenous markers, will improve Indigenous peoples' lot in life. Settler logics of native elimination continue to manifest in the lives of Indigenous migrants from Latin America, Speed argues, when they cross into the United States and are interpolated through their national identities (e.g., "Mexican" or

"Guatemalan") rather than as members of Indigenous communities. For Indigenous migrants who do not speak Spanish, this interpolation can prove deadly as demonstrated by the deaths of Indigenous peoples at the hands of American law and border enforcement.[54] While the U.S. settler state may refuse or choose to not acknowledge their Indigeneity, once in the United States, Indigenous migrants must also contend with prejudice from some non-Indigenous Latinxs, who recognize their Indigeneity and discriminate against them because of the negative connotations associated with Indigenous peoples in Latin America. In the process of migration, then, U.S. and Latin American structures of class, race, and Indigeneity hybridize and create what Blackwell conceptualizes as hybrid hegemonies.[55]

Solagueño Migrations

While anthropologists have long studied Indigenous peoples, the sites in which Indigenous peoples are studied have shifted as a result of globalization and neoliberal policies that have displaced thousands of Indigenous peoples from their communities of origin and forced them to migrate to the U.S. for a chance at survival.[56] The distinct experiences of Indigenous immigrants, however, are often conflated with the experiences of their *mestizo* (people of mixed Indigenous and Spanish ancestry) counterparts in state records and in academic work.[57] Nevertheless, scholarly work has shown that Indigenous immigrants' racial background not only is at the root of their displacement, but also influences the nature of their social lives in the U.S. and their interactions with their co-nationals and members of the Latinx community.[58] Until recently, research on Indigenous migration focused almost exclusively on the experiences of first-generation immigrants with little to no discussion of their U.S.-born children. Yet the lived experiences of the children of Indigenous immigrants offer a unique vantage point from which to see how migration across settler borders transforms processes of Indigenous self-making among displaced Indigenous peoples.

Many of the diasporic Solagueño youths I interviewed are, like myself, the grandchildren or great-grandchildren of braceros—men who migrated to the United States as part of the Bracero Program, a guest worker program that brought Mexican nationals to the United States from 1942 to 1964.

Thus, for many of us, the first people in our families to migrate to the United States did so with authorization. Such opportunities were not available for our parents, the children and grandchildren of Solagueño braceros. Solagueño braceros worked on farms and eventually returned to Solaga at the end of their contracts. In Mexico, the 1940s and 1950s were marked by the international migration of some Indigenous groups, including the P'urépechas of Michoacán and Mixtecs and Zapotecs from Oaxaca.[59] Scholars trace this pattern of international migration from Mexico to the United States to contemporaneous changes in these countries, including the economic modernization of Mexico that displaced people from their lands and traditional forms of subsistence at the turn of the twentieth century; the integration of the American Southwest into the national economy, which created a demand for workers; and a labor shortage as a result of World War II.[60] At that time, American policy geared toward Mexico reflected the countries' interdependent needs. For instance, the Bracero Program gave landless Mexicans employment and remedied the American labor shortage.

The recruitment of Indigenous men for the Bracero Program, some scholars argue, was another attempt by the Mexican state to assimilate its Indigenous population. Solagueños and other Indigenous immigrants who participated in the Bracero Program diversified the Mexican migrant population, since the majority of men who participated in the program prior to the recruitment of Indigenous men had been *mestizos*.[61] The Mexican state saw the Bracero Program as an opportunity to integrate the Indigenous population into the Mexican nation.[62] Indigenous Mexicans who participated in the Bracero Program could return as Spanish-speaking *mestizos*, having relinquished their Indigenous languages and dress. This logic not only reflects the Mexican state's nationalist agenda but also how Mexico and its *mestizo* population imagined Mexico's Indigenous peoples: as static, monolingual, and in need of modernization. *Mestizo* braceros stereotyped Solagueño braceros as a result of their Indigenous background. While my great-grandfather was a monolingual Zapotec-speaker, an ideal candidate for the Mexican state's assimilationist program, this was not the case for all Solagueño braceros. Don Nicolás, a bracero I interviewed, remembered an exchange he had with another bracero who realized he could read when he saw him diligently checking his pay stub. He recalled the *mestizo* Mexican's shock that an Indigenous person could read and write. Don Nicolás laughed as he delivered the punchline to his story: in the end, the man asked him to read letters from his family in Mexico and to check his pay stub every week to ensure he was fairly compensated for his labor. Don Nicolás found it humorous that he, who had previously been ridiculed because of his Indigenous background, became integral to this bracero's migration project. Don Nicolás's experience demonstrates how the Mexican state and *mestizo* braceros engaged racial stereotypes and hierarchies about Indigenous peoples and how these have informed Solagueño migrant experiences from the beginning of international migration.

While Don Nicolás, my great-grandfather, and other braceros eventually returned to Solaga, their children and grandchildren would be forced to emigrate from their hometown decades later albeit without the protection of a guestworker program. As Jonathan Xavier Inda observes, the end of the Bracero Program helped spark the flow of unauthorized migrants from Mexico.[63] Despite the termination of the program and the backlash from the influx of Mexican immigrants in the United States, there was still a demand for migrant labor.[64] Furthermore, the transportation, communication, and human infrastructure built to transport braceros to the U.S. facilitated the movement of undocumented migrants. Importantly, the recruitment of Mexican men for the Bracero Program established a relationship between Mexico and the United States, as well as a pattern of circular migration, in which men would work in the U.S. for a short period, make money, and go back to their hometown.[65] The end of the Bracero Program, however, foreclosed an avenue through which Solagueños and their Mexican compatriots could migrate to the U.S. with authorization.

While Solagueño men participated in the Bracero Program, they were part of the small fraction of transnational Oaxacans migrants since most Oaxacan migrants opted to stay within Mexican territory.[66] Indigenous Mexican displacement in the twentieth century, researchers argue, is marked by three moments: intraregional movement for seasonal work in the 1940s and 1950s, migration to cities and agro-export zones in the 1960s and 1970s, and migration to northern Mexico and to the United States with the rise of neoliberalism in the 1980s and 1990s.[67] During the 1960s and 1970s, Oaxacans migrated to coastal plantations for seasonal work, to cities for wage

labor, or to areas where there was contract work for state projects. Their displacement was driven by the Mexican government's agrarian policy, which
privileged large-scale irrigation projects rather than subsistence farming;
the price controls that lowered the market value of maize; and the increasing availability of jobs in Mexico's urban centers.[68] Impacted by these crises
and finding themselves unable to make ends meet in their hometown as
subsistence farmers in the 1960s and 1970s, Solagueños migrated to Oaxaca
City and Mexico City in search of employment. Some Solagueños settled in
these cities, while others decided to venture to the United States. Don Mauricio shared his experience as one of the first Solagueños to migrate and
eventually settle in Los Angeles in the 1970s. Without the social network
on which subsequent generations of Solagueño immigrants relied upon
arriving in Los Angeles, Don Mauricio struggled to find work. Don Mauricio and his *compadre* Cristobal, also from Solaga, eventually found work
at a restaurant in the Westwood area of Los Angeles where they worked as
butchers until the location went out of business. Finding themselves jobless
after two years in the U.S., they decided to return to Solaga. While Don
Mauricio did not fare too well during his first trip to Los Angeles, he eventually returned to Los Angeles and encouraged others to try their luck in
the U.S. In fact, many of Solaga's first transnational migrants would return
to their hometown, assemble a group of Solagueños who wanted to make
the journey to the U.S., and depart for the United States. As in other Indigenous communities, migration became a common strategy through which
individuals, families, and communities sought economic well-being.[69]

When Don Mauricio made his way to Los Angeles a second time, he
found his *paisano* Lucas relying on work from a temp agency. Lucas first
migrated from Solaga to Mexico City and later made his way to Los Angeles. His arrival in Los Angeles was integral to Solagueños' entry into the
dry-cleaning industry. His experience operating a dry-cleaning business
in Mexico City gave him the skills necessary to work in this sector in Los
Angeles. As a result, dry-cleaning became an immigrant niche occupation, in which Solagueños used their social networks to learn their trade
and find employment. Hometown networks facilitated Solagueños' entry
into the dry-cleaning industry and made it easy for potential employers to
find workers using these same networks. During his search for work his first

time in Los Angeles, Don Mauricio stumbled upon a dry-cleaning business looking for workers. Recalling this and Don Lucas's experience in this industry, Don Mauricio persuaded Lucas to leave his work at the temp agency to go into dry-cleaning in Los Angeles.

While Don Mauricio did not have the skills necessary to work in the dry-cleaning industry, Lucas's arrival in Los Angeles provided Don Mauricio and other Solagueño immigrants with a niche industry in which they could work. With an established network of Solagueños at dry-cleaning businesses, future waves of Solagueño immigrants had an easier time finding jobs. Solagueños working at dry cleaners across Los Angeles taught new Solagueño arrivals how to use industrial machines to iron clothing, which they called "yendo a la práctica," or going to practice. Once they learned their trade, Solagueños would start working at other dry-cleaning businesses. While the promise of a higher wage persuaded Don Lucas and other Solagueño immigrants to work in dry-cleaning, their wages were and are still relatively low. The pay rate among dry-cleaning workers within the Solagueño community still varies according to legal status, with undocumented workers often making less than documented workers, as in most industries. Research has shown that working conditions are worse for undocumented workers vis-à-vis their documented counterparts.[70] In addition, the jobs available to undocumented workers are less likely to give them access to sick days, overtime, and health benefits.[71] Dry-cleaning also has little room for promotion. For instance, if individuals enter the industry as pressers, as most Solagueños do, they likely remain in that position. Solagueños' work as pressers in dry-cleaning businesses is also physically grueling. Many Solagueños began working in these positions as teenagers or young adults. As they grow older, they are less likely to be hired as pressers or are given only part-time work. Still, many strive to own their own dry-cleaning businesses, but few are able to so.[72] Importantly, although working in this physically demanding sector may structure Solagueño lives, it does not define or consume Solagueño existence. Indeed, Solagueños' ancestral way of life connects them to a world where they are more than commodified labor. For this reason, *The Children of Solaga* focuses on *el goce comunal*, or the communal joy Solagueños engage in through the spaces they have created to celebrate their hometown and communal identities in diaspora.

Soy de un pueblo alegre

Extensive research has focused on Oaxacan migration. This work includes research on identity formation among first-generation Oaxacan immigrants in the U.S., the living and working conditions of Oaxacan immigrants, as well as research on the effects of transnational migration on traditional social, religious, and political structures in their Indigenous sending communities.[73] Kearney and Stephen found that Oaxacans' Indigenous background makes them targets of discrimination by non-Indigenous Mexicans in both Mexico and the U.S., and by some in the dominant U.S. population. Stephen has also documented the changes migration has brought to Oaxacan migrants' communities, including changes to social and cultural institutions and how migration has also transformed sociopolitical and cultural organization for migrants living in the U.S., where they have formed hometown associations and have begun to organize under pan-ethnic organizations. Through these organizations, Fox and Rivera-Salgado add, Oaxacan immigrants draw on their ancestral practices, affirm their collective identities, and connect with their communities of origin in spite of anti-Indigenous discrimination at the hands of Mexican co-nationals.

My work extends this rich body of work by focusing on the transborder lives and practices of the *children* of Indigenous immigrants, paying particular attention to how youth have become central to diasporic Solagueño community life. Rather than framing Indigenous experiences in terms of binaries (e.g., Solagueño *or* Mexican identities and Indigenous *or* modern) and reinscribing ideas about Indigenous people as static that occlude Mexican efforts to assimilate them, *The Children of Solaga* recognizes the fluidity of Oaxacans' identities. Contrary to scholars' supposition that Oaxacan immigrants would be unsuccessful in their efforts to transmit their cultural practices to their children,[74] this book demonstrates that they have been so successful in these endeavors that their children have become indispensable to the reproduction of Indigenous Oaxacan community life in the United States.

The extensive literature on Oaxacan migration reflect a history of displacement of Indigenous peoples from Oaxaca. More recent work on Indigenous Oaxacan migration demonstrates that Indigenous migrants' experiences continue to be shaped by racial inequalities. Seth Holmes's

Fresh Fruit, Broken Bodies discusses the structural and racial inequality Triqui immigrants experience in agricultural farms and how these inequalities become normalized. Holmes describes his work as an "ethnography of suffering" and suggests that Triquis are forced to migrate to escape slow, communal death in their communities of origin.[75] Indeed, recent works on Indigenous migration detail the increasingly difficult conditions Indigenous peoples endure in their countries of origin, including state and police violence, economic exploitation, and racial discrimination, and how these lead them to migrate to the United States in increasing numbers.[76] Lauren Heidbrink's *Migranthood* discusses the effects of U.S. and foreign intervention on Indigenous Guatemalans, who have resorted to migration as a collective and historically rooted survival strategy against racism, historical violence, and intergenerational structural inequality in Guatemala. *Migranthood* complicates the narrative that the arrival of 70,000 Central American children at the U.S.-Mexico border in 2014 was an unprecedented humanitarian crisis. Instead, Heidbrink argues, it was in fact a policy crisis long in the making and largely a result of U.S. economic and political intervention in Central America.[77] Shannon Speed's *Incarcerated Stories* delves into the interpersonal and state violence that Indigenous women from Mexico and Central America endure before, during, and after their migration to the United States. Speed argues that neoliberal economic and political policies make Indigenous women vulnerable to violence. This violence is continuously reinforced by settler-imposed racial and gender ideologies.[78]

The aforementioned texts study Indigenous migrants in transit. Speed notes that this focus distinguishes her own work from previous work on Indigenous immigrants, which tend to center immigrants who settled in the U.S. These texts, however, focus on the experiences of first-generation Indigenous immigrants and take their informants' Indigenous identity as a given. The children of Indigenous immigrants differ from their parents' generation because, for the most part, they no longer possess the traditional markers by which people are labeled as Indigenous, including living in an Indigenous town or speaking an Indigenous language. Thus, *The Children of Solaga* shows how children and youth construct and negotiate their Indigenous identities with their racial, ethnic, community, and national identities away from their ancestral homeland. Written by a member of the community being studied, *The Children of Solaga* delivers a nuanced take on the lives of Indigenous immigrants and their children with attention toward Indigenous resistance and resurgence. While we undoubtedly experience pain, we are still capable of joy.

The Children of Solaga focuses on joy for two reasons. First and foremost, a focus on joy is a nod toward Indigenous futurity and a shift from a focus on the pain we experience as Indigenous peoples.[79] Despite multiple and continuous attempts to eradicate our cultures, our communities and identities persist. The fact that Solagueños have reappropriated practices rooted in colonization and transformed them into joyous ways to transmit their cultural and community values across generations and borders is not to be dismissed. Second, such a reclamation of joy is part of "the work we do to reclaim our whole, happy, and satisfiable selves from the impacts, delusions, and limitations of oppression and/or supremacy."[80] While *The Children of Solaga* focuses on joy, the marginalization Indigenous Latinxs and other marginalized peoples experience in their homelands and abroad undoubtedly shape how they navigate the world. When our Indigenous identities are stigmatized across space, time, and generation to rejoice in who we are and where we come from is the most revolutionary and transformative act of all.

During the course of my fieldwork, I often found myself in tears. These tears, however, were tears of joy. I was in awe that despite Mexican and American assimilationist projects and the anti-Indigenous discrimination Solagueños have encountered for multiple generations, Solagueños remained undeterred. Diasporic Solagueño children and youth's participation in the band and traditional *danzas,* as well as their incorporation of Solagueño culture into rites of passage like *quinceañeras,* demonstrated their connection to and pride in their Indigenous culture. *The Children of Solaga* strives to capture the joy and fulfillment Solagueños experience across generations through their participation in communal life.

The Children of Solaga reflects *el goce comunal,* or the communal joy diasporic Solagueños experience through their communal practices, particularly from celebrations in honor of their community's patron saints. Following Mixe and Zapotec thinkers, I understand *fiestas* and the communal enjoyment of *fiestas* as acts of resistance.[81] While scholars have reduced *fiestas* to social and economic leveling mechanisms in Indigenous communities,[82] Indigenous Oaxacans emphasize the role of *fiestas* in bringing a *pueblo* together to stage celebrations, share in the fruits of their collective labor, renew their collective hopes, and reaffirm the collective.[83] *Fiestas* can only occur through an engagement in communal practices of belonging through which Solagueños claim belonging across generations and borders. Importantly, an emphasis on engagement in communal practices highlights that for Indigenous scholars and community members, belonging is not predicated on residing in an Indigenous community, speaking an Indigenous language, or wearing traditional attire.

While written in a romantic context, Mixe songwriter and musician Honorio Cano's song, "Soy de un pueblo alegre," articulates the fallacy in thinking that Indigenous peoples' lives are enveloped by suffering when we have so much to celebrate, including our provenance in *pueblos alegres*, or joyous communities. Cano's song has become part of a vast musical repertoire in Oaxaca's Sierra Juarez and its diaspora. This repertoire includes *sones* and *jarabes*, classical or orchestral pieces, religious *cantos*, and popular Mexican *cumbias*, *boleros*, and *norteño* music. Most of the music Serrano bands perform does not have lyrics. With the contemporary rise of songs penned in Spanish or Indigenous languages spoken in the region, including Cano's songs, some bands now also sing when they perform these songs. Solagueño musicians, or *wekuell*, are renowned for their musicianship among Serranos. Over generations, they have developed a distinct sound that memorializes the *maestros* that have influenced what diasporic *wekuell* call the "Solaga style," a style of playing that has become associated with their homeland. Solagueño *wekuell* maintain this unique sound across borders, and in doing so allow us as Solagueños to rejoice and take pride in our distinct communal and sonic identities.

To experience *el goce comunal* is to "await the *fiesta* anxiously, to experience it how you want to experience it, and to reminisce about it when it's over," one community member, Isaac, told me. For Isaac, communal joy is ephemeral and idiosyncratic, yet annual patron saint celebrations set the stage for Solagueños who now live in different places to come together in celebration of their communal identity across time, generation, and, as a result of displacement, across borders. Settler states not only have constructed a world where Indigenous peoples must migrate for their own and their collective survival, but also have instituted systems of domination in which Indigenous identities are stigmatized. Through their sonic practices, young musicians create a space and a means through which their diasporic community can mediate the alienation these systems of domination engender. *Fiestas* and Indigenous practices of belonging through which *fiestas* are organized provide a haven for Solagueños and their children to be connected with their ancestors, their *paisanos*, and with their ancestral homeland.

Chapter Overview

Chapter 1 discusses the cultural and historical settings of my research sites and situates the book in the ethnographic record on Oaxacan communities in Mexico and the United States. In doing so, I detail anthropological work on the *cargo* system in Mesoamerica, an Indigenous institution that organizes social, political, and ritual life and defines membership in Indigenous communities, and examine how transnational migration has transformed the *cargo* system and other aspects of Oaxacan community life. This chapter departs from scholarly conceptualization of the *cargo* system as a punitive system that maintains social and economic equilibrium in Indigenous communities and instead focuses on the *cargo* system as the political aspect of what Indigenous scholars have conceptualized as *comunalidad*, an Indigenous way of knowing and being in the world through which individuals demonstrate belonging to their community. I shift the focus from the political to the social sphere of *comunalidad* and focus on patron saint celebrations or *fiestas*. I explore the community-building aspects of *fiestas* embedded in the cost-sharing efforts, *fiesta*-specific *cargos*, and *mayordomía* (sponsorship) that are necessary to stage these celebrations. Importantly, Solagueño immigrants have adapted elements of *comunalidad* to their lives in diaspora by fulfilling their political obligations to their *pueblo* through hometown associations and have maintained and created community ties through patron saint celebrations. While the *cargo* system has been adapted to the transborder lives of Solagueño immigrants, their U.S.-born children form their community identities away from the community and out of the purview of the *cargo* system. Thus, diasporic Solagueño youth must rely on millennial forms of belonging, like participation in *fiestas*, while creating new ways to demonstrate their attachment and claim belonging to their ancestral homeland.

In Chapter 2, I examine the larger social context of Oaxacan immigrant lives in Los Angeles, California, focusing on the Solagueño immigrant experience. I discuss the migration of Solagueños from their hometown in Mexico to Los Angeles, including the areas in which they settled and their relationships with individuals from neighboring Serrano communities. This chapter engages with studies on immigrant incorporation and assimilation by analyzing how the social and economic conditions Solagueños encounter in the receiving community affect immigrants and their children, as well as how immigrants leave impressions on the communities in which they reside. In this context, Indigenous children and youth form their racial, ethnic, and national identities. Solagueños and their children are interpolated as Mexican and Latinxs, groups that have been constructed as "illegal aliens." Nevertheless, members of the Latinx and Mexican immigrant populations may discriminate against Oaxacans for being Indigenous. *Mestizo* youth my interlocutors encountered succinctly summarized racial tropes about Indigenous people by pointing out that Oaxacan youth were "short, dark, and ugly." While Solagueños' national, racial, and ethnic identities mark them as Other, the concentration of Oaxacan immigrants in the Mid-City and Koreatown neighborhoods of Los Angeles has brought about a vibrant Oaxacan community, in which diasporic Indigenous children and youth grow up alongside each other and in which Oaxacan immigrants can transmit aspects of their culture and values to their children through celebrations for their hometowns' patron saints.

Chapter 3 delves into the significance of return trips for 1.5-generation and second-generation Solagueños. This chapter centers the notion of *convivencia*, which I characterize as the practice of living and engaging with people and place through which Indigenous peoples form, maintain, and demonstrate belonging to their community. This chapter considers *convivencia* as the catalyst for diasporic return trips: Solagueño immigrants encourage their children to embark on return trips to the home community so they can live in and engage with their *pueblo*. Through *convivencia* in the ancestral homeland, diasporic children and youth are able to experience their Indigenous culture in the flesh. The appreciation they gain for their *pueblo*, its culture, and its way of life may encourage them to build and maintain relations with Solaga and its people. Migration, however, has brought about potential obstacles to *convivencia*, including the necessity of legal documentation to return to the home community, as well as cultural and linguistic differences that arise from living in diaspora. Nevertheless, the relationships children and youth build with and in Solaga encourage them to continue returning to their homeland and influence diasporic community life in Los Angeles.

Chapter 4 highlights the role of diasporic Solagueño musicians in creating the sonic space through which Serranos, people from Oaxaca's Sierra Juarez region, and Solagueños can affirm and build a communal sense of belonging. Through soundscapes that include music, language, and sounds associated with their hometowns, Serranos engage in and show belonging through millennial and ever-evolving forms of Indigenous communal life. Centering autochthonous modalities of communication (including voice, music, and dance) through which Indigenous peoples construct their social world, challenges Western traditions that have historically privileged the written word to dismiss Indigenous communicative practices. For Zapotec peoples, Zapotec thought, dance, and spiritual practices are embedded within musical expressions. So too is the landscape of their homeland. For Indigenous peoples living in diaspora, the aural, or what we hear, has the capacity to transform the reality of what we see. Thus, while they may not be able to be physically present in their communities, Serranos in "separate spaces can savor the same sounds."[84] Music allows youth to form and sustain ties to their communities of origin and to create spaces in which Indigenous immigrants can transmit their cultural and community values to their children away from their homeland. In processes of identity formation for diasporic Solagueño youth in Los Angeles, communal practices allow Indigenous youth to connect their places of settlement with their places of origin. The deterritorialization and reterritorialization of Oaxacan aural practices allow Indigenous immigrants and their children to replenish their Indigenous identities away from their ethnic homeland despite living in anti-immigrant and anti-Indigenous settler colonial contexts.

The concluding chapter synthesizes the research findings and discusses the significance of this study to the discipline of anthropology, work on migration, and studies of Indigeneity and Latinidad.

ONE

The *Cargo* System and Indigenous Belonging

FOR MANY CHILDREN OF Solagueños born in diaspora, like myself, Solaga has been ever-present. Solaga exists in the language many of our parents speak, the food we eat, and the pride in our hometown with which we are instilled despite living away from our ancestral homeland. For those of us who grew up in the 1990s, Solaga also existed in the videotapes our relatives in Solaga sent to our families in Los Angeles after every patron saint celebration. These videos allowed those of us born in diaspora a glimpse into the world our parents left behind in their search for a "better life."[1] In my case, Domingo's video collection allowed me a glimpse into my first experience of that world over two decades earlier. *Fiesta* videos allowed our parents, most of whom were undocumented, to engage in the communal enjoyment of their hometown festivities even when their legal status in the United States impeded their physical presence in their community of origin.

Patron saint celebrations were occasions Solagueño migrants chose to return to their hometown during the first two decades of Solagueño transnational migration. These visits allowed Solagueños to bring the goods they bought and remittances they earned back to their hometown. Some of these trips also allowed transnational migrants to recruit other community members who wanted to make their way to the United States. In this way, Solagueño transnational migration was cyclical from the outset; that is, community members worked in the United States for a period of time and returned to their community of origin, often repeating this pattern according to their community's ritual calendar. As crossing the border without authorization—the only option for Indigenous migrants whose racial and economic background has long hindered opportunities for authorized migration—became increasingly dangerous, videotapes allowed Solagueños in Los Angeles to stay connected to their hometown.

Eduardo, a 31-year-old member of the 1.5 generation who was born in Oaxaca and brought to the United States as a child, reminisced about watching *fiesta* videos and their significance for his family:

> I remember seeing videotapes because people were bringing videotapes. So that was a whole week. Like Friday night, "we're watching the first part" and it took like ... oh my god ... so many hours on one event! Saturday we'd watch the second part, Sunday you were like, "Okay, play it again, play it again," but now as I look back, my parents wanted to stay connected to it.

The 1990s were a significant decade for Solagueños and other immigrant communities in the United States. As the decade progressed, opportunities to cross the border without authorization and adjust one's status if in the United States without authorization became more difficult. During this period, Solagueño cyclical migration was essentially halted and the Solagueño community was divided by the increasingly difficult-to-cross border. In this context, video recordings of *fiestas* became increasingly important. Solagueños who returned to their hometown and were able to make their way back to the United States brought with them videotape sets containing hours of footage of *danzas*, *jaripeo*, donations, and *bailes* staged in honor of the community's patron saints. The need for Solagueños to stay connected to their hometown and its festivities, which Eduardo pointed out, is rooted in the ways in which participation in the staging and celebration of patron saint festivities are ways in which Solagueños have appropriated European-imposed institutions as practices through which community members demonstrate community belonging and transmit their cultural and community values across generations.

This chapter departs from scholarly conceptualizations of the *cargo* system, an Indigenous institution that organizes social, political, and ritual life and defines membership in Mesoamerican communities, as a punitive system that maintains social and economic equilibrium in Indigenous communities. Instead, in this book I focus on the *cargo* system and patron saint celebrations as practices of *comunalidad* through which Solagueños determine and claim belonging to their community. In doing so, I draw on scholarship on *comunalidad,* a set of practices and way of knowing and being in the world through which Indigenous Oaxacans demonstrate belonging to their community.[2] Scholars have divided *comunalidad* into four fundamental principles or pillars: communal authority, communal labor, communal territory, and communal joy.[3] I shift the focus from the *cargo* system, or the political sphere of *comunalidad,* to the social sphere of *comunalidad* and focus on patron saint celebrations or *fiestas.* As the manifestation of the fourth pillar of the philosophy of *comunalidad, fiestas* represent a space of communal joy through which community members share in the fruits of their labor, renew their collective hopes, and create a space in which communal identity and belonging can be strengthened and solidified.[4] Most importantly, *fiestas* allow Solagueños to experience *el goce comunal,* or the celebration of our collective identity and our communal way life. I explore the community-building aspects of *fiestas* embedded in the cost-sharing efforts, *fiesta*-specific *cargos,* and *mayordomía* (sponsorship) that are necessary to stage these celebrations. Importantly, Oaxacan immigrants have adapted elements of *comunalidad* to their lives in diaspora by fulfilling their political obligations to their *pueblo* through hometown associations and maintaining and creating community social ties through their participation in patron saint celebrations.[5] While the *cargo* system has been adapted to the transborder lives of Solagueño immigrants, their U.S.-born children form their community identities away from their parents' hometown and out of the purview of the *cargo* system. Thus, diasporic Solagueño youth must rely on millennial forms of belonging anchored in the social sphere of *comunalidad* and create new ways to demonstrate their attachment and claim belonging to their ancestral homeland.

Colonial Origins of the Cult of the Saints in Latin America

Festivities honoring patron saints have become central to Solagueño life across generations and borders. Patron saint celebrations not only structure ritual time in Solaga and other Indigenous communities, but also provide a structure through which the community can come together and celebrate their hometown. Participation in patron saint celebrations is built into the civil, political, and religious organization of the community, the *cargo* system, which was first instituted in Mesoamerican communities after the Spanish conquest of Mexico.

The veneration of saints in Latin America is deeply intertwined with the region's colonial past. Patron saint celebrations are festivities held in honor of Catholic saints who were appointed as the protectors of certain causes, vocations, or institutions.[6] Spanish conquistadors imposed the Catholic cult of the saints on the so-called New World, forcibly converting the Indigenous population. Indigenous towns were renamed with the names of saints, which mapped the new religious order onto the newly conquered territory. Conquistadors also dispossessed Indigenous peoples from their ancestral lands and placed them into Spanish-created towns to facilitate their evangelization and give Spaniards access to their forced labor and tribute.[7] The designation of patron saints for specific Indigenous communities not only gave communities a common object of devotion, it also marked a period of time during which a community and its neighbors gathered to celebrate the saints.[8] In our community's case, *Zoolaga* was renamed San Andrés Solaga and community members now celebrate the feast of our namesake San Andrés, or Saint Andrew, each year on November 30, as well as *La Virgen del Carmen* on July 16.

In their attempts to convert the Indigenous population, Spanish missionaries also appropriated pre-Hispanic rituals, dances, and music, incorporating them into Catholic celebrations and the civil-religious calendar of Indigenous communities. Due to a sizable multiethnic Indigenous population with different religious ideologies, however, the missionaries' conversion efforts in colonial Oaxaca were largely superficial. In the Sierra Juarez mountain range of Oaxaca, where Solaga is located, colonial records show that Indigenous communities used Catholic celebrations as a pretense to bring community members together for ritual sacrifices to ask for "prosperity, good health, and good harvests."[9] These records reflect that those communities and individuals who were caught participating in these rituals were severely punished and often whipped. Ultimately, colonial religious and civil authorities were successful in tapping into and modifying preexisting community practices by establishing the *cargo* system and a Catholic calendar that emphasizes the celebration of patron saints.

Scholars have posited that the *cargo* system and patron saint celebrations serve various functions in Indigenous communites. Some argue that sponsorship of these celebrations serves as a leveling mechanism by which wealthier members of Indigenous communities can display their wealth through acceptable channels.[10] Others have written about patron saint celebrations as a social glue that brings Indigenous communities together and contributes to the production and reproduction of these communities.[11] While these religious celebrations may originally have been institutionalized as a means of colonial control over Indigenous people, in what follows, I contend that in their current form they allow the Solagueño community in Solaga and abroad to gather and reproduce their community and its traditions, generating a sense of belonging and joy among its participants.

Evangelization of Indigeneous Oaxacans

In Oaxaca, the task of evangelizing the Indigenous population fell to the Dominican order. Often outnumbered and unable to visit the scattered Indigenous communities, Dominican friars used the figures of saints as a tool for Christianization.[12] Dominican friars represented Catholic saints as figures similar to Zapotec deities. The sixteenth-century Iberian veneration of Catholic saints did indeed share some commonalities with native beliefs. For Serrano Zapotecs, worshiping community-specific beings in the figure of Catholic saints was more akin to their religious practices than worshiping a single Christian God.[13] Like their Zapotec counterparts, saints had human needs and attributes and could intercede with a higher supernatural being on behalf of humans to ensure the welfare of their community. While the similarities between Zapotec deities and saints facilitated conversion efforts, the Catholic clergy tried to control syncretic forms of worship in Indigenous communities. Sierra Norte communities continued to hold secret ceremonies worshiping their pre-Hispanic deities into the eighteenth century.[14] Rather than a celebration of saints, Chance argues that these festivities became "much more than religious occasions; they were also celebrations of community identity, power, and prestige vis-à-vis other communities. ... As time went on and affection for the saints (perhaps syncretized with Indigenous community ancestors) increased, Catholic *fiestas* gradually came to express a collective community identity in much the same way as the pagan ceremonies had before."[15] While patron saint celebrations began as a Spanish imposition, Indigenous communities in the Sierra Norte reappropriated these celebrations and maintained aspects of their pre-Hispanic traditions and identities in syncretized religious practices and new forms of social organization. I argue that Solagueño patron saint celebrations continue to be celebrations of a collective community identity. Furthermore, the practices that emerged from organizing patron saint celebrations, including *fiesta*-specific *cargos* and sponsorships, have become a way for Solagueños across place and generation to show belonging to their community.

Anthropological Studies of the *Cargo* System

Along with the imposition of Catholicism, Spanish authorities instituted a new form of governance in Indigenous communities in the Sierra Norte, which became known as the *cargo* system. This new form of governance was based on Iberian concepts of community governance and relied on a local council, or *cabildo*, of officials, which included "a *gobernador*, one *regidor* (councilman), one *alcalde* (judge), one *mayor* (a police chief who functioned much as the previous alguaciles), an *escribano* (scribe), and a *fiscal* (a servant of the church who was responsible to the local priest)."[16] *Cabildo* officials were elected and ratified every year. Conflict usually arose when Spanish authorities refused to ratify the officials chosen by the communities. Disputes also arose among community members, particularly those descended from or who claimed to descend from noble Indigenous lineages. If elected to lower-ranking *cargos*, these men would refuse to serve the *cargo* and take their case to court. This refusal went against the egalitarian structure of the *cargo* system: when men came of age they were expected to first serve in the lower-ranking *cargos*, eventually working their way up to more prestigious, higher-ranking positions. When Indigenous nobility became obsolete toward the middle of the eighteenth century, Chance argues, the *cargo* system became the mechanism through which Indigenous men sought prestige in their communities.[17]

In the 1950s, anthropologists conducted extensive research on *cargo* systems in Mesoamerica, drawing different conclusions as to the function of the *cargo* system in societies that were then characterized as "closed corporate communities."[18] Scholars characterized these communities as mono-ethnic, averse to change, disapproving of the accumulation and display of wealth, and prone to reducing the effects of wealth accumulation on the communal structure.[19] In contrast, open communities were comprised of a multiethnic population that continuously interacted with the outside world, changed according to outside demands, and permitted and expected individual accumulation and displays of wealth.[20] In closed corporate communities, scholars argued, religious *cargos* allowed wealthier individuals to gain prestige and display and redistribute wealth within the community in a socially acceptable manner.[21] Sponsorship of patron saint celebrations through the *cargo* system allowed Indigenous communities to maintain equilibrium in their societies by preventing individuals from accumulating too much wealth relative to other community members.[22] In addition to a mechanism through which Indigenous people are kept impoverished, the *cargo* system has also been interpreted as a way to keep Mexico's Indigenous population separate from the *mestizo* population, people of mixed Indigenous and Spanish origin.[23] Because fulfilling a *cargo* required physical presence in the community, leaving the community or refusing to fulfill a *cargo* meant renouncing membership in the community, as well as access to the community's natural resources, communally owned land, and the right to own a home and be buried in the town.[24] For scholars ascribing to these interpretations of the *cargo* system, participating in the *cargo* system and organizing *fiestas* under the *cargo* system made Indigenous people complicit in their own oppression.[25]

More recent work on the *cargo* system discusses changes in the system resulting from transnational migration and the rise in Protestantism in Indigenous communities.[26] These changes include Indigenous communities having migrants designate a replacement to serve the *cargo* on their behalf, requiring their migrant population to send annual payments to their communities in exchange for the communal labor requirements they are unable to fulfill while living abroad, or temporarily relieving migrants from service with the expectation they will resume their service upon their return to the community.[27] Also explored is the impact of Protestant refusal to contribute money or labor for patron saint celebrations. In particular, conflict with Protestant converts demonstrates how deeply intertwined religious and civic practices are in Indigenous communities like Solaga. Not assuming a *cargo* position because of religious differences puts community members in danger of losing the right to live in or hold property in the community. Community members may see a refusal to fulfill a *cargo* as an affront because those who do not take on *cargos* may expect to remain a part of the community and benefit from a communal way of life without assuming the same responsibilities as community members who do fulfill their *cargos*.[28] For immigrants, not fulfilling a *cargo* through the mechanisms the community has created to account for emigration could also affect their ability to return to their home community when they would like to.

While scholarly critiques of the *cargo* system and patron saint celebrations may be valid according to context, as Whitecotton notes:

> Religion, to the extent that it provided yet another focus for strong Indian community solidarity in the face of pressures from within and without, also provided an important psychological function for the Indian. Fiestas held in conjunction with the cult of saints, became a time when Indians could escape the tensions of everyday life, of poverty, of alienation, and of strong pressures to become submerged in a tightly knit social unity as well as a time to dream of utopias.[29]

For Solagueños and other Indigenous peoples, the annual festivities in honor of their patron saints designate a time and place where the community comes together. Thus, community members are not only paying homage to and celebrating the saints, they are also paying homage to and celebrating their own community.[30] Following Whitecotton's observations, I posit that patron saint celebrations allow Solagueños to demonstrate their ties to Solaga. By providing a space through which Solagueños can experience communal joy, I later argue, *fiestas* also provide diasporic Solagueños with a reprieve from the marginalization they experience as a result of their Indigenous background. To scholarly discussions on the *cargo* system, I add how the fixed yet flexible nature of *fiestas* allows local Solagueños to show belonging with their contributions to the staging of patron saint celebrations through *fiesta*-specific offices in the *cargo* system and allows diasporic Solagueños to also show their devotion to their hometown as *mayordomos*, or sponsors for the *fiesta*. The joy and satisfaction *mayordomos* get from their contribution allows us all to rejoice in *el goce comunal*.

Comunalidad

I draw on scholarship on *comunalidad* to demonstrate the importance that Serranos, Indigenous people from the Sierra Norte of Oaxaca, place on communal life and communal practices in their homeland and in diaspora. Floriberto Díaz and Jaime Martínez Luna, Mixtec and Zapotec intellectuals, are credited with developing *comunalidad*, a concept that attempts to explain the nature of communal living in Indigenous societies.[31] For Martínez Luna, *comunalidad* functions as a way of life for Serrano communities and essentially a reason for being.[32] The universal principles and truths about Indigenous societies encompassed by *comunalidad*, Díaz argues, allow us to understand Indigenous existence.[33] These scholars' understanding of "Indigenous identity as something that is based on what individuals *do* for the community and not on physical, biological, and linguistic traits" challenges essentialist notions of Indigeneity that assume physical, biological, and linguistic characteristics.[34]

Díaz and other thinkers divide *comunalidad* into four fundamental principles or pillars:

1. communal authority (as seen in general assemblies through which communities make decisions and nominate or appoint individuals for positions in the *cargo* system);
2. communal labor (unremunerated work in service of the community through *tequio* and the *gozona*, or collective work on community projects and mutual aid, respectively);
3. communal territory (a collective space in which communal living is enacted); and
4. communal joy (the enjoyment or celebration of the ritual cycle through patron saint celebrations and the reproduction of communal life).[35]

Notably, *comunalidad* incorporates Indigenous notions of communal living, as well as communal institutions that arose out of colonization and evangelization, namely the *cargo* system and patron saint celebrations.

While the amalgamation of European and Indigenous practices may be interpreted as exemplary of syncretism, Martínez Luna interprets the form of governance that emerged from these colonial impositions as a form of Indigenous resistance, particularly in the ways in which communities have responded to Spanish-imposed institutions with their own ways of thinking and organizing.[36] The political sphere of *comunalidad* consists of rotating *cargos* or civil-religious positions that organize social, political, and ritual life. Unlike anthropological scholarship on the *cargo* system that regarded this institution as a leveling mechanism meant to maintain equilibrium in Indigenous societies by preventing the individual accumulation of wealth,[37] scholarship on *comunalidad* understands the *cargo* system as an egalitarian institution through which all townspeople, as part of the community's general assembly, nominate or appoint individuals for positions in the *cargo* system.[38] In fulfilling these *cargos*, individuals serve their community and, in doing so, establish community membership. Service to the community, as a means of establishing community membership, ensures that anyone can be integrated into the community so long as they are willing to participate in communal institutions, that is, the general assembly, the *cargo* system, and *tequio*.[39] The *cargo* system, then, has become an institution through which Serranos ensure the survival of their communal way of life.[40]

Community members' physical presence in the communal territory, or town, is integral to the function of local governance and communal living.[41] As Aquino Moreschi points out, if community members are physically absent from the hometown, they are unable to fill *cargo* offices or practice other aspects of *comunalidad*. As such, emigration from Indigenous communities may present a challenge for *comunalidad*.[42] The Zapotec community of San Jeronimo Zoochina, for instance, feared their town and their way of life would disappear as a result of a period of heavy emigration in the 1970s. Nevertheless, diasporic Zoochinenses consistently return to their community to ensure that it remains inhabited. In Los Angeles, they also partake in cultural, social, and political practices through which they maintain, create, and re-create identity and belonging, a process Brenda Nicolas identifies as transborder *comunalidad*.[43]

As an epistemology and practice, *comunalidad* was conceptualized as rooted in a shared territory.[44] However, Nicolas's research demonstrates that *comunalidad* can be and is practiced outside of the communal territory.[45] While holding *cargo* office may no longer be plausible for many Serranos in diaspora, they continue to partake in *comunalidad* in and outside of their hometown despite their physical absence from their hometown. The continuity of diasporic communal practices ensures that Serranos' ways of knowing and understanding the world are transmitted to their children in diaspora. Solagueños in the 1990s used return trips for *fiestas* and later *fiesta* videos, like Eduardo and his family, to maintain a connection with their hometown. As crossing the U.S.-Mexico border became increasingly difficult, moreover, Solagueños began celebrating their community's patron saints in Los Angeles, incorporating the aspects of the celebrations that they could adapt to life in metropolitan Los Angeles. It is no accident that many of the practices that Serrano communities maintain in diaspora center patron saint celebrations. These events not only draw community members of all ages but also center Indigenous ways of knowing and being in the world, thereby allowing for the maintenance and establishment of community ties and for the transmission of Indigenous knowledge to children and youth who grow up or are born in diaspora, as I discuss in Chapters 3 and 4.

Fiestas incorporate Serrano ways of being and knowing the world and also establish community membership. From a young age, Solagueños participate in the staging of patron saint celebrations; as children and youth, for example, they are asked to or volunteer to participate in *danzas*, or choreographed dances performed over the course of their town's *fiesta*. As they mature, they will likely organize *fiestas* as officeholders in the community's *cargo* system or may choose to sponsor items or events for the celebrations.[46] Others join the community's municipal band and partake in communal life as musicians. In partaking in *fiestas*, Serranos engage in the social sphere of *comunalidad* or the philosophy of *goce* (enjoyment) within *comunalidad*.[47] These concepts recognize the labor that goes into organizing community celebrations, as well as the joy and fulfillment community members get from *fiestas* as the outcome of their shared labor. Through *fiestas*, community members can support and celebrate their community. Throughout this book, I engage in this sphere of *comunalidad.*

While Solaga has *fiesta*-specific *cargos* and committees to organize the town's two major patron saint celebrations, officeholders and committee members also rely on community member contributions.[48] Some of these contributions are mandatory, while others are voluntary. Solagueño households, for instance, are required to contribute *tortillas* to feed visitors at *la casa de la comisión,* the building on the edge of town where community members and visitors dine during patron saint celebrations. Additionally, in the weeks leading up to these celebrations, members of the *comisión de festejos* (celebration comission) visit every Solagueño household to collect donations of staple foods, including coffee, corn, beans, and *panela*, as well as monetary donations. These donations are recorded by committee members and announced following the festivities. It is in the spirit of these cost-sharing practices, I argue, that diasporic Solagueños can continue to show their dedication to their community despite living outside of the home community and out of the purview of the *cargo* system, an institution that has long been a mechanism to demonstrate belonging in Indigenous communities.

Solagueño cost-sharing efforts vary from other Indigenous employments of cost-sharing systems, in which *mayordomos* (sponsors) collect money or other goods from fellow townspeople to stage a celebration rather than shouldering the costs themselves.[49] Through this cost-sharing system, communities can continue holding *fiestas* despite declining interest in sponsoring these celebrations as a result of a shift toward a more individualistic mentality among community members.[50] In these communities, however, individual sponsorship was first the norm, whereas in Solaga, cost-sharing efforts have been the norm. Through the donation of foodstuffs, participation in *danzas*, and assisting *cargo* holders and mayordomos in the staging of these festivities, among other forms of participation, Solagueños work together to host celebrations. In Solaga, individual sponsorship of patron saint celebrations (or aspects of these festivities) is a relatively new phenomenon that stems from transnational migration. The aforementioned donations from Solagueño locals are modest in comparison to the items and monetary donations diasporic Solagueños are able to afford. Still, diasporic Solagueños who can and cannot physically return for patron saint celebrations rely on their friends and family to assist them with their sponsorship through the *gozona*, a system of reciprocity and mutual aid that promotes collective cooperation and unites community members at the individual, familial, and community levels.[51] In this instance, a *mayordomo* will reap the *gozona* that they or their family has sown through assisting other community members with their own social or ritual obligations in the community. Those community members will now support them to ensure the success of their *mayordomía*. Through *mayordomía* practices, Solagueños who are physically absent from their community can still engage with their *pueblo* and cultivate interpersonal and communal bonds to show belonging to their community.[52]

El goce comunal

While *The Children of Solaga* centers *comunalidad* as it unfolds in *fiesta* settings, Solagueños engage in communal labor (the *gozona* and *tequio*) outside of *fiestas* year-round. The communal enjoyment of *fiestas*, then, is the shared satisfaction in and celebration of the fruits of this collective way of life.[53] Importantly, participation in communal life allows Serranos to connect with our ancestral way of life as we reckon with our incorporation into Western societies as commodified labor, a way of life we have had to adopt for our collective survival. *Fiestas*, much like our way of life, are oriented toward a collective understanding of the world rather than an individualistic approach to the world. Indeed, the incommensurability between Indigenous and Western ways of understanding the world may be why outsiders who observe and even partake in our *fiestas* fail to understand the logic behind these celebrations.[54] As Caballero and Ríos Morales note, people may find it surprising that Indigenous communities "squander" their income to contribute to a single moment of these celebrations.[55] While Indigenous people are affected by processes of globalization, "the circulation of money without the search for its accumulation continues to be a principle that still governs" our communities' patron saint celebrations.[56] Rather than a socially acceptable mechanism to redistribute wealth in our communities, as previous scholars have argued, *fiestas* are moments in which Solagueños share their wealth, no matter how big or small, for the enjoyment of the community. This is both a celebration of the community and a way of showing belonging through our communal practices.

Community members participate in *fiestas*, Isaac, a Oaxaca City–born Solagueño, explained, "because they have an identity deeply rooted in that community and they enjoy it. *El goce comunal* is tied to identity ... that you *feel* like you are a part of it."[57] Partaking in and enjoying a *fiesta*, Isaac suggests, reinforces community members' connection to their *pueblo*. To belong to Solaga is to know or experience *el goce comunal*; to find joy in the celebration of our community or who we are and where we come from. Isaac's explanation of belonging to Solaga and arguably belonging to an Indigenous community more broadly rejects settler state notions of Indigeneity that function to dismiss identity claims for Indigenous peoples who do not reside in an Indigenous community, speak an Indigenous language, or wear traditional attire. This autochthonous conceptualization of Indigenous belonging is more attuned to Indigenous ways of knowing and being in the world that recognize the importance of community members' participation in *el goce comunal* as an aspect of *comunalidad*.

Our experience of *el goce comunal* would not be possible without Solagueños' willingness to come together to stage patron saint celebrations and to share what they can with their *pueblo* despite already living with limited economic resources. Isaac attributes Oaxacans' fondness for *fiestas* to the large Indigenous presence in this state. I asked Isaac to elaborate on why he thought Oaxacans liked to organize *fiestas*. He responded, "because we're *fiesteros* ... for everything." Isaac proceeded to explain a Lenten tradition in Oaxaca City, in which store owners leave out pots of water for passersby in remembrance of Jesus's exchange with a Samaritan woman. In doing so, he discussed Oaxacans' propensity to share what little they have:

> There are businesses that, I mean, are very modest but they give it to you from the bottom of their hearts. They give water and I take it and receive it from the bottom of my heart because people give it like that. Imagine. Why

do they do it? It's a big expense but because they want to share. I mean who in the world? I mean where in the world?

Isaac pointed out how counterintuitive it may seem for small store owners to take on this big expenditure. I shared with Isaac that I had noticed Solagueños' willingness to share. Every time you enter a Solagueño home, for example, you are offered food and drink. If you refuse, it is perceived as rude. When I arrive in Solaga and begin my rounds of visiting friends and family, I know I must prepare to eat and drink at every home. Food and beverage may be as modest as a cup of *agua fresca* or coffee, or as large as a whole meal. During *fiestas*, Solagueños also engage in this practice, inviting visiting revelers, strangers and friends alike, into their homes to eat with them during the celebrations. This generosity is one of the reasons that Solaga is known for its hospitality. Isaac's story made me think that perhaps this was common among all Oaxacans.

He proceeded to tell me how he saw this generosity and communal spirit play out in Solaga:

> At the community level, I lived it with my grandparents. When my grandfather died, I was there. Are you kidding me? When people arrived! I mean they came with all their heart to help ... to get stuff from the kitchen. They come and give you things because they feel moved to come and give you things. I mean with my grandmother, who helped a lot of people to make food, a lot of people arrived ... with *cooperación* or with firewood, beans. They were there helping. The *tortilleras*! That's hard work. Why? I've said it in different spaces that a funeral is the space where you most see ... what do you want to call it? The *mano vuelta, tequio, gozona*. One time someone passed away that didn't live in Solaga and my cousin's wife tells me, "She's coming from Oaxaca. Nah! Well, she's not here. She didn't help." I mean they have this mentality that they're coming from the outside. They don't know them or simply the person was indifferent [to the community]. Right? To prove my point: when my grandmother or my grandfather died, people went. "Well, *la tía* helped me at some point" or "She was a good person" and that part is where you feel the support ... not just financial but spiritual and emotional.

Isaac linked *fiestas* with the way of life that makes communal existence possible. In his example, Isaac's grandmother is an ideal Solagueña: in life, she was an active community member who contributed to the community through her culinary expertise. Her participation in communal life was rewarded with the financial, spiritual, and emotional support her *paisanos* provided for her family after she passed. On the other hand, Solagueños will not render the same support to the family of a deceased person who is perceived as being indifferent or uninvolved in the community. In a setting where community membership hinges on participation in communal life, diasporic Solagueños must find creative ways to establish community membership outside of the purview of the *cargo* system and quotidian life in the community.

Diasporic Solagueño Participation in *el goce comunal*

Restrictive immigration policies and border enforcement have made it harder for undocumented immigrants to engage in circular migration.[58] The increasingly difficult task of crossing the U.S.-Mexico border has greatly limited return visits, changing cyclical patterns of Solagueño migration in which community members would leave their hometown for work and return for patron saint celebrations. Don Anibal, a 68-year-old Solagueño living in Solaga whose three children migrated to the United States, remembered how Solagueños who had migrated to Oaxaca City and Mexico City began the practice of returning to Solaga for patron saint celebrations:

> The people that would return had only gone to Mexico and Oaxaca. With migration to the United States, everything completely changed. Before, they could go and come back. They just needed money to cross. Not like now, it's more dangerous. People can't just go like they used to without papers. They went, they came back, they went, they came back. They would just come back for the *fiesta*. Sometimes they would stay.

As a community member, Don Anibal witnessed the shift from urban migration to transnational migration within the community and, through his children's experiences, the differences between internal and transnational migrants, mainly how difficult return trips became for Solagueños who had to cross the U.S.-Mexico border.

While crossing the border has always been a dangerous endeavor, the militarization of the U.S.-Mexico border has made this undertaking even more life-threatening. Nevertheless, Solagueños living in Los Angeles, including those living in the United States without authorization, engage in return visits when they are able. Don Anibal believed Solagueños return to the hometown because "they do not forget their *pueblo*. They are proud of where they come from. They want the chance to be able to spend time with their relatives." Perla, who migrated to the United States as a teenager and returned to Solaga to sponsor a *fiesta* despite her undocumented status, believed that Solagueños return to their hometown for patron saint celebrations because "it doesn't feel the same to be here [in Los Angeles], than to be there [in Solaga]." Don Anibal's and Perla's remarks echo the importance of communal territory and communal enjoyment in the shared territory embedded in *comunalidad*. They also capture the importance Solagueños place on being physically present *in* their community and the longing Solagueños feel to be in their homeland when they are unable to partake in *el goce comunal* and to *convivir* with their community, that is, to live and engage with and form and cultivate bonds with their *pueblo* during patron saint celebrations, as I write about in Chapter 3. While Solagueños have begun celebrating their patron saints in diaspora, Perla notes, these *feel* different from the festivities in Solaga. When experienced in the community, Martínez Luna posits, *fiestas* bring about a confluence of feelings and bodily sensations, including feelings of enjoyment and well-being, distraction, satisfaction, and fatigue from participating in and organizing these celebrations.[59] Part of the satisfaction that Serranos draw from *fiestas* comes from the assurance their community gets from knowing they put on a good celebration. Thus, Solagueños must work together to put on these celebrations and ensure the community puts its best foot forward.

Don Anibal explained how *cargo* holders, individuals who are responsible for organizing the celebrations under the *cargo* system, and *mayordomos*, individuals who choose to be sponsors, work together to feed visitors during the *fiesta*:

> The *comisión de festejos* has the biggest responsibility, since they feed visitors and there are usually a lot of people. They must ensure the *pueblo*

doesn't look bad. From there, it's people's personal choice what they will give. My son, for example, gave a bull and our neighbors gave another. [The bulls] are donated specifically for [*la casa de la comisión*]. It's the *pueblo*'s custom for the nourishment of visitors.

According to Don Anibal, the *comisión de festejos* bears the greatest responsibility since they must feed visitors three meals a day at *la casa de la comisión*. Solagueños pride themselves on their hospitality, often boasting that once visitors experience the *fiesta* in Solaga, they will surely return. Visitors, who include visiting musicians, athletes, and revelers from surrounding communities, will take with them not only memories of the festivities and our *goce*, but also how well they were treated and, in Don Anibal's estimation, how well they were fed at *la casa de la comisión*. In order to live up to the expectations visitors and Solagueños alike have of Solaga, *cargo* holders, *mayordomos*, and the community at large must work together to put on a successful *fiesta*. While the *comisión de festejos* takes care of the logistics, townspeople like Don Anibal's son and their neighbors provide donations to help with one aspect of these elaborate celebrations. These men, both of whom are first-generation immigrants living in Los Angeles, donated bulls to be slaughtered for their meat. I posit that the aforementioned sponsors and diasporic Solagueños living in Los Angeles take on *mayordomías* not only because they can more easily assume the financial undertaking that these involve, but also because *mayordomías* provide diasporic Solagueños an opportunity to demonstrate belonging when they are no longer able to engage in everyday practices of *comunalidad*, including unrenumerated communal labor and service through the *cargo* system.

Mayordomías are sponsorships of celebrations in honor of a community's patron saints.[60] In some Indigenous communities, individuals may choose to sponsor *mayordomías* to show gratitude to a patron saint for their support in curing an illness or their success in business.[61] In other Indigenous communities, community members take on religious *mayordomías* in lieu of providing civil service in the community through the *cargo* system.[62] While these *mayordomos* may spend a considerable amount of money, Joo notes, assuming these positions allows a person to fulfill obligatory communal service without consuming their labor and time in civil *cargo* positions where their tenure may last one to three years. Other Indigenous

Oaxacan communities require individuals to sponsor *mayordomías*, which may prove financially burdensome for some community members. While there are religious or *fiesta*-specific offices in the Solagueño *cargo* system, religious *cargo* holders are not responsible for financing *fiestas*. They may, however, rely on their social networks to raise funds for aspects of the *fiesta* that fall under their position's purview.

Migration has also brought changes to *mayordomías* in Indigenous communities, particularly the meaning attached to sponsoring *mayordomías*. In his research in Santa Ana del Valle, Jeffrey Cohen found that 2 percent of the community's households designated a portion of immigrant remittances to sponsor *mayordomías*. While only a small fraction of immigrant remittances may be allocated to *mayordomías*, the motives of immigrants and immigrant families to sponsor patron saint celebrations may shed light on the "symbolic and cultural frames including values, customs, and communal cultural tradition within which migration takes place."[63] By using remittances to sponsor *fiestas*, Joo argues, immigrants can intensify their networks with community members and maintain a sense of belonging even though they live far from home. Similarly, I argue that *mayordomías* provide diasporic Solagueños an opportunity to contribute to *el goce comunal* (communal enjoyment) and to demonstrate belonging to their community when they are no longer able to work in the community to stage these celebrations through institutions and practices that were available to them when they were physically present in the community. While *mayordomía* does not require the sponsor's direct presence in the community, a sponsor's friends and families may help in aspects of the sponsorship that require physical presence, such as feeding visiting bands or purchasing flowers and candles to use in religious celebrations. In some cases, undocumented Solagueños may even send their U.S.-born children to Solaga as their representatives. Through these return visits or by watching videos of these celebrations, as in Eduardo's household, diasporic Solagueño children and youth come to understand the importance of remaining connected to their community through patron saint celebrations and may choose to engage in these practices by continuing to travel to their parents' hometown for these festivities or becoming *mayordomos* themselves as they reach adulthood.

Comunalidad in Diaspora

Migration has brought changes to Indigenous communities and the institutions through which they have determined belonging. Indigenous immigrants create ingenious alternatives to institutions of belonging that necessitate physical presence in order to remain connected to their communities of origin. No longer able to participate in their town's *cargo* system, diasporic Solagueños formed hometown associations through which they support and maintain ties with their community.[64] Unable to experience their hometown celebrations in the flesh, displaced Solagueños used video recordings to mediate displacement. As Eduardo's childhood memories demonstrate, watching *fiesta* videos became its own event for Solagueños. For almost two decades, engaging with patron saint celebrations through video recordings was the only means through which Solagueños in Los Angeles could experience their town's *fiestas* until the formation of the Los Angeles–based Solagueño youth band in the early 2000s. As I demonstrate in the chapters that follow, music has allowed diasporic Solagueño children and youth to form and sustain ties to their communities of origin and to create spaces in which Indigenous immigrants can engage in communal enjoyment and transmit their cultural and community values to their children away from their homeland.

As an Indigenous epistemology and practice, *comunalidad* was conceptualized as rooted in a shared territory and arguably tied to systems of governance that emerged from colonization. Diasporic communal life among Serranos demonstrates how Serranos continue to partake in aspects of *comunalidad* away from their homelands and outside of Indigenous institutions through which they have come to show belonging. As they began celebrating their town's patron saints in Los Angeles, Solagueños and their children, particularly those who became musicians in the Solagueño youth band, closely engaged with cultural, social, and political practices through which they now maintain or re-create identity and belonging. Nicolas identifies this process as transborder *comunalidad* and argues that "everyday practices of Indigenous culture, language, and social and political ways of being" allow Indigenous Oaxacans to contest Indigenous erasure and to resist multiple forms of state violence that seek

Indigenous elimination.[65] In diaspora, these practices become critical to Indigenous Oaxacans because they are interpolated as Mexican nationals in the United States and, in this process, their distinct Indigenous identities are erased. Despite the erasure of their Indigenous identities by the U.S. state, Indigenous Oaxacans continue to experience discrimination at the hands of *mestizo* Mexicans and non-Indigenous Latinxs because of their Indigenous origins.[66] As a result, community spaces in which Serranos celebrate their communal identities and practices provide Indigenous youth with a space to celebrate their culture; these settings have transformed how Indigenous children and youth form their identities in diaspora. Rather than rely on videotapes to experience their hometown festivities, Solagueños can now experience these celebrations in Los Angeles. While patron saint celebrations in Los Angeles might not elicit the same feelings as those in Solaga, they create a space in which Solagueños can model *comunalidad* for their children.

Isaac noted how diasporic Solagueños, like myself, are able to experience *el goce comunal* through the Indigenous practices of belonging that Solagueños maintain in diaspora and the *convivencia* the children of Solagueños foster during return trips:

> In Los Angeles, people are deeply connected to *fiestas*, the bands, the food because they [your parents] take the culture over there and because of that you all come back and because you enjoy it. Like you were saying right now, "Well, I'm coming back in July. I'm going to do this … I'm going to the *recua* … the *jaripeo*" because you also feel that belonging and you feel part of [the community].

In Isaac's estimation, the experience of *el goce comunal* in Los Angeles serves as the spark that leads diasporic children and youth to want to return to their ancestral homeland where they come to develop a sense of belonging by living and engaging in and with their *pueblo*. Once there, many of us experience a sense of joy and belonging that connects us to our *pueblo* and our ancestors.

As I describe in the previous chapter, my first trip to Solaga predates the establishment of Solaga's Los Angeles–based band. My memories of this trip are sparse and at times mediated by media. So too are my memories of my family. Living on the U.S. side of the border meant that I did not physically meet my family in Oaxaca until I was 5 years old. Instead, my grandparents and I met through the pictures and videos that were able to travel across the border my parents and grandparents could not (or were not supposed to) cross.[67] My favorite family photograph captures *da Pach Pio,* my grandfather, mid-*grito* dancing to a *jarabe* with my grandmother. His ecstatic face shows how thrilled he is in that moment.[68] While I cannot pinpoint the exact moment in which the picture was taken, I have often imagined his *grito* or joyous shout was a result of the band playing his favorite *jarabe,* "La Hermanita," or perhaps it was the joy he felt dancing with my grandmother. I had not been able to articulate why this was my favorite picture of him until the penning of this book: it shows my grandfather *en pleno goce comunal.*[69]

This memento captured one of the many moments in which my grandfather experienced the ecstasy of the celebration of being in and with his *pueblo.*[70] A video captured me with a similar expression during the *Virgen del Carmen calenda* in July 2022. That summer, Solaga's municipal authorities lifted restrictions that limited access to the community during the coronavirus pandemic. Three years after the last *fiesta* in honor of *La Virgen del Carmen,* diasporic Solagueños were finally able to return to the community. Thus, when someone shouted *"¡Que viva San Andrés Solaga!"* ("Long live San Andrés Solaga!") during the *jarabe* my friend and I were dancing, my joy and our communal joy was undeniable. We were once again in our ancestral homeland dancing in celebration of our communal way of life and our collective identity.

Every time a band begins to play "La Hermanita" and men shout to express their delight, I remember the joy in my grandfather's expression. While I was never able to experience a *fiesta* with him after my first trip to Solaga in 1995, his and my grandmother's memory lives on. I taught their great-grandson, who was born in the U.S., how to dance *jarabes* during the *calenda* in honor of *La Virgen del Carmen* held in 2023. After ten minutes of coaching him through the steps, he embarrassedly asked me how long the songs lasted. When I told him we probably had another twenty minutes to go, he looked shocked. I told him we could stop dancing, but he powered through the *jarabe.* When the band transitioned into "La Hermanita," I shared how much his great-grandfather loved that *jarabe.* He immediately lit up. My nephew had recently started asking my cousin about our deceased relatives. I could not share too much about my grandfather since I barely knew him. This fact, however, meant a lot to my nephew. In that moment, my nephew and I connected with our ancestors through music and dance and reveled in the *goce* they once experienced with our *paisanos* in our ancestral homeland.

Conclusion

The festivities honoring patron saints have been central to Solagueño communal life in the home community and are now central to maintaining and establishing community membership across borders and generations. Patron saint celebrations not only structure ritual time in Solaga and other Indigenous communities, but also provide a structure through which the community can come together and celebrate their hometown. Participation in patron saint celebrations is built into the civil, political, and religious organization of the community—the *cargo* system—and Solagueños are able to partake in these celebrations through individual sponsorships. Through these contributions and later the creation of a Los Angeles–based band, diasporic Solagueños have managed not only to mediate their displacement from the home community, but also to create new ways to demonstrate their and their children's attachment to their ancestral homeland. In staging and participating in community events, Solagueño immigrants act on a sense of responsibility for their *pueblo* and demonstrate their willingness to continue being part of the community[71] in diaspora. This enactment of *comunalidad* allows Solagueños to fulfill an obligation to the community and show belonging to the collective.[72] Instilling this ethic in the next generation is integral for the social reproduction of Indigenous communal life. While these practices were modeled for Solagueños since their childhood in their hometown, they continue to embrace and engage them, allowing their children to learn and decide whether they too will engage in *comunalidad*. These practices are especially significant for diasporic Solagueños whose identities are under assault in two settler contexts that erase Indigenous peoples from their social landscapes and national imaginaries and promote assimilation as part of their nation-building projects. If Indigenous peoples and non-White immigrants relinquish their cultures, Mexican and American settler states have long assured them, they will eventually integrate into the national fold. *The Children of Solaga* demonstrates that rather than rejecting their Indigeneity and relinquishing Indigenous practices of belonging, diasporic Solagueños have embraced them and used them as a way to mediate their marginalization on both sides of the U.S.-Mexico border.

TWO

Home of the Oaxacans

ONE AFTERNOON BEFORE FRIDAY night band practice, I picked up Matias from the apartment building where he lived with his parents and siblings. A junior at Alexander Hamilton High School's Academy of Music and Performing Arts, Matias had already made the seven-mile trek from his school on the Westside of Los Angeles to his home in Koreatown. Despite the hour-long commute on public transportation, Matias was his usual animated self. When we had arranged our interview, he asked me to pick him up so we could grab dinner and talk before we headed to band practice. Like many people from Solaga, Matias and I are biological cousins. Thus, as he pointed out in the statement that follows, it was not uncommon for us to hang out. We ended up at a taco place down the street from the rehearsal space in which *Banda Juvenil Solaga USA,* our hometown's youth brass band, held practice.

In between taking bites from his burrito, Matias observed:

Growing up in Los Angeles there's a lot of Koreans because it's Koreatown ... in Los Angeles there's a lot of Oaxacans. Like the area is a lot of Solagans.[1] They live in the Valley, Downtown, but mostly in Koreatown. So it's just ... since we all live so near each other ... us ... the cousins[2] ... the kids ... the Solagans ... hang out and also the schools are filled with Oaxacans. They might not be Solagans, but they're Oaxacans. All my friends from elementary, they're all Oaxacan and we didn't realize it until we met each other's parents and we're like, "Oh snaaaap! You're Oaxacan?

I didn't even know that!" Also, the high schools. Like Hamilton to me is "Home of the Oaxacans" not "Home of the Yankees" 'cuz there's so many Oaxacans there.

With his words, Matias, then 16 years old, drew a map of Solagueño Los Angeles and described how Indigenous Oaxacan immigrants moved into and subsequently changed established neighborhoods thereby altering the racial geographies of Los Angeles. These racialized geographies are informed by the erasure and displacement of the Tongva, Los Angeles's first inhabitants; settler colonial fantasies of a White utopia; the forced relocation of American Indians; the Great Migration of Blacks from the American South; White flight; and post-1965 international migration. As Matias suggests, Koreatown continues to be a popular enclave among South Korean immigrants in Los Angeles, and while Koreans may not necessarily reside in the area, it continues to be populated with Korean businesses.[3] Oaxacans have created strong communities within this ethnic enclave, and Serranos, individuals from the Sierra Norte region where Solaga is located, account for the largest Oaxacan community in Los Angeles.[4] The concentration of Oaxacans in Koreatown has allowed the children of Solagueños to foster a strong sense of community with other diasporic Solagueño and Serrano children and youth. While these encounters may begin in neighborhood schools, Oaxacan youth redefine their relationship with space and disrupt the racialized geographies of Los Angeles in ways that were not accessible to previous Solagueño generations. As students, Solagueño youth inhabit identities and breach spaces where their parents are permitted only as laborers and where they are treated as if they were invisible.[5] During our conversation, Matias noted how his teachers associated Oaxacan students' origins with musicianship. For Oaxacan youth who as *bi wekuell*, or musicians, fill the ranks of their *pueblos'* bands in Los Angeles, this assumption rings true. Matias, a musician in Hamilton's jazz band and *Solaga USA*, is able to transform the Westside from a site of exploited labor for Serrano immigrants to a site where Indigenous artistry is acknowledged and celebrated. Furthermore, in declaring Hamilton High School to be "Home of the Oaxacans," Matias not only alludes to the changing demographics of the school but challenges settler iconography that erases Indigenous peoples, including the Tongva, the original peoples of the Los Angeles basin, and Indigenous immigrants from Latin America, from landmarks, monuments, and histories of Los Angeles.[6]

The image of Founding Father Alexander Hamilton and the use of the Yankee as a school mascot tap into settler grammars that not only erase the original peoples of Los Angeles but also make it difficult for non-White immigrants to claim belonging in territories in which they have a legal birthright to citizenship.[7] In the United States, Solagueños and their children are interpolated as Mexicans and Latinxs, groups that have been constructed as "illegal aliens." The assumption that people of Mexican origin, regardless of nascency, are in the United States without authorization and "thus illegitimate members of society undeserving of social benefits, including citizenship"[8] sets them apart from the descendants of White immigrants who are believed to have more "legitimate" claims to citizenship. In a context where Indigenous Oaxacans are excluded in their country of origin and in the country to which they migrated because of their ethnic, racial, and national background, designating a school as "Home of the Oaxacans" can be read as an attempt to create a sense of place in a space where such a claim is otherwise denied.

As students and musicians, diasporic Solagueño youth challenge and redefine the spatial boundaries of Indigenous Los Angeles. Diasporic Solagueño youth are able to find a sense of home through the relationships they establish with their Oaxacan peers, through their participation in their Indigenous community life, and through the external validation they may receive from non-Indigenous educators as a result of their artistry. In this chapter, I examine the racialized geographies to which Solagueño immigrants arrived in Los Angeles and how Indigenous Oaxacans' presence in Los Angeles has altered the geographies of Los Angeles to the point where the children of Solagueños can redefine their schools and the city as "Home of the Oaxacans." While discrimination may be intrinsic to the everyday lives of Solagueño immigrants and their children, community spaces provide diasporic children and youth with a space where their culture is celebrated. These spaces have transformed Solagueño communal life across borders and how Indigenous youth form their identities in diaspora.

Race and Place in Los Angeles

As the children of displaced Indigenous peoples living in the United States, Solagueño children and youth confront Latin American and U.S. structures of coloniality and racial domination, a phenomenon that Blackwell describes as hybrid hegemonies.[9] The legacy of Spanish, Mexican, and Anglo colonization is inscribed on the very land Solagueños now call home. While the territories from which and to which Solagueños migrated were under different colonial jurisdictions at different moments, the settler societies that emerged in these places effectively erased Indigenous peoples from the social landscape and later the national imaginary. Matias's engagement with his school's iconography speaks to this erasure. Through its name and mascot, Hamilton High School celebrates the figure of "Founding Father" Alexander Hamilton, an immigrant from the West Indies, and perpetuates the idea that the United States is a White, immigrant nation. The children of Indigenous immigrants from Latin America, like Matias, are socialized into settler grammars, or "discursive logics that maintain settler colonial ideologies,"[10] through their schooling. These narratives replicate settler colonial logics of erasure and elimination that deny the continued existence of Indigenous peoples or make U.S. Native Americans the antagonist of American national mythology and posit that Indigenous people perished altogether and European settlers arrived on vacant land.[11] White settlers, then, construct themselves as the new "natives" and structure belonging through racial hierarchies that acknowledge and privilege them as the first settlers and the group most entitled to citizenship.[12]

While some Indigenous Latinx children may recognize the commonalities between their Indigenous communities and native North Americans in the brief instances they appear in social studies curricula, some may not or may choose not to associate themselves with U.S. Native Americans for fear of being associated with peoples deemed to be the villains of U.S. national mythology.[13] Matias's claim that his high school is "Home of the Oaxacans" may be interpreted as another instance of Indigenous Oaxacans being complicit with the City of Los Angeles's multicultural agenda that occasionally celebrates Oaxacan immigrants and simultaneously erases the continued presence of the Tongva.[14] However, how Indigenous youth understand themselves within overlapping settler projects demonstrates not only the effectiveness of these projects but how they continue to shape Indigenous peoples' everyday lives and senses of self. In other words, Matias's declaration reflects the settler grammars through which the children of Indigenous Latinx immigrants are socialized and attempt to make sense of their place in their schools, among Latinxs, and in U.S. society.

In the 1970s, Solagueños arrived in a place where settlers had long used different technologies to erase and contain Indigenous peoples.[15] California missions were sites where Spanish colonizers attempted to forcibly assimilate native peoples by eradicating their way of life.[16] Spanish priests separated California Mission Indians from their families and cultural teachings, including ceremonial telling and singing.[17] By separating unmarried girls and women from men within missions and locking them in dormitories at night, Kelly Lytle Hernández argues, missionaries conducted the first experiment of human caging in the Tongva basin.[18] In separating native peoples from their land, settlers attempted to separate them from their culture and to limit their mobility. These efforts continued as Spanish families began settling *El Pueblo de Nuestra Señora la Reina de los Ángeles sobre el Río Porciúncula*, a town that neighbored the Tongva village of Yaanga.[19] Spaniards instituted the *casta* system, which determined an individual's caste based on their race, culture, and socioeconomic status, with Spaniards positioned at the top, followed by mixed-race individuals, and "Indians" and Africans at the bottom.[20]

Under this racialized hierarchy, Indigenous peoples were classified as minors and made wards of the Catholic church and the Spanish state. Considered *gente sin razón,* or people without reason, Native "lawbreakers" endured corporal punishment at the hands of Spanish authorities who considered them incapable of adjusting to the colonial order without physical punishment.[21] These unequal power dynamics were exacerbated by the ecological devastation colonists wreaked in Yaanga and eventually made Tongva natives economically dependent on Spanish colonists. Spanish settlers in turn used this economic dependency to justify their rule over Native peoples.[22]

While the Mexican War of Independence was partially fought to bring about the end of the *casta* system, the legacy of this racial order remained.

Despite the equal status men were afforded as citizens of the new Mexican republic, newly "Mexican" Angelenos used "law, custom, trickery, and violence to create and invest with meaning alleged differences between themselves and Indians."[23] Their efforts ensured historically marginalized "others" remained at the bottom of the social order albeit on the basis of criminalized activities rather than the "innate" racial differences put forth by the *casta* system.[24] Natives who were arrested for being unemployed, for example, were forced to pay a fine or sentenced to labor on public projects or for private employers. This arrangement institutionalized the forced labor of Native peoples and marginalized others whose way of life conflicted with that of the Mexican Californios. In addition to purported differing lifestyles, Mexican Californios "made racial judgments based on a nexus of factors, including behavior, dress, status, and ancestry"[25] to distinguish between themselves and the Tongva who through intermarriage were phenotypically similar to Mexican Californios. Anglo settlers, however, arrived in Los Angeles with their own racial categories, which they would eventually impose on Angelenos—one that asserted Mexican Californios' mixed ancestry made them incapable of self-governance.

While Anglos and Mexican Californios managed to coexist when Anglos first migrated to Los Angeles, once the United States annexed Los Angeles, Anglo social, economic, and legal traditions gained traction.[26] While the Treaty of Guadalupe Hidalgo legally classified former Mexican citizens as "White," Anglo racial ideas posited that Mexican Californios were not truly White and were in fact "racially brown, economically backward, and culturally impoverished."[27] Racial tropes previously used against Native peoples in Los Angeles were now used on Mexican Californios to similar ends. Anglo settlers would eventually institute similar technologies of containment first used on Native peoples on their Californio counterparts in an effort to transform Los Angeles into a White settler paradise.[28] This resulted in the mass incarceration of groups of people that destroyed this settler fantasy and the containment of groups deemed unworthy of living in the White settler paradise into other areas of the city. Mexican Californios would become indistinguishable from recently arrived Mexican immigrants, and people of Mexican origin as a whole would be and continue to be cast as permanently foreign, regardless of citizenship status.[29]

These ideas about race and place inform the racial logics and geographies of the Los Angeles in which Solagueños arrived, the histories of the city taught to Angeleno youth, and consequently how diasporic Indigenous youth see themselves and their communities within the city.

Solagueño Arrivals

The infrastructural changes made by Anglo settlers once they assumed power in the latter half of the nineteenth century had lasting effects on the city in which Solagueños arrived. In his history of Los Angeles, Torres-Rouff describes how the shift of space and water from communal responsibilites to private commodities under Anglo settlers would come to reflect the inequalities inscribed in Los Angeles's Anglo foundations.[30] In 1870s Los Angeles, these inequalities were manifested in the lack of sewers and paved streets in the areas in which non-Whites resided. These inequities continued into the twentieth century with zoning laws concentrating industrial activity (and the resultant environmental pollution) in non-White and immigrant areas of the city, including South Central Los Angeles.[31] At the same time, affluent Whites moved to suburban communities where they were threatened by neither industrial activity nor the presence of non-Whites. When Solagueños and other immigrants from Latin America arrived in Los Angeles in the 1970s, South Central had already been shaped by industrialization, the migration of poor Whites from the American South (who worked in these industries), Black migration from the South, and subsequently White flight.[32] Like other Black and Latinx working-class communities in the 1980s and early 1990s, Solagueños experienced Los Angeles "as a space of a deindustrialization marked by migration, incarceration, and evisceration of the social wage."[33] The shared experiences ultimately culminated in the conditions that would eventually lead to the 1992 Los Angeles uprising, as well as coalition building between Black and Brown communities.[34]

As Laura Pulido notes, the geography of past racial regimes informs immigrant settlement patterns, as does the need for affordable and accessible housing.[35] As a result of low incomes, a third of immigrant families settle in central city neighborhoods, which are deemed less desirable places to live.[36] Scholars note that living in these areas exposes immigrants and their children to gangs, drugs, and crime that could set them on a path toward downward assimilation, that is, dropping from their parents' social position as immigrants to an even lower social class.[37] Framed differently, Blacks and Latinxs living in central city neighborhoods are targets of racist policies, including overpolicing, surveillance, and employment discrimination, all factors which may make them susceptible to incarceration.[38] Coupled with environmental racism and disinvestment in communities of color, phenomena that are less common in majority White neighborhoods, Indigenous Latinx immigrants and their Black and non-Indigenous Latinx counterparts are spatially bound to areas of Los Angeles that are by design "sites of poverty and pathos."[39] Notwithstanding these conditions, people of color in these neighborhoods have established vibrant communities whose social scenes have produced new identities, identifications, and coalitions.[40]

Lucas and Marina were among the first Solagueños to settle in Los Angeles in the late 1970s. Their two-bedroom apartment in the neighborhood of South Central served as a landing pad for Solagueños when they arrived in Los Angeles. Along with Lucas, Marina, and their two children, Solagueño newcomers, my parents included, resided in this two-bedroom apartment until they found jobs and made enough money to move to their own apartments. South Central Los Angeles of the 1980s and 1990s was described as "comprised of economically impoverished enclaves that are plagued by high unemployment and underemployment, crime, gang violence, drug and alcohol abuse, dilapidated housing, high educational dropout rates."[41] Lucas and Marina considered their neighborhood to be so dangerous that they would not allow their children to play outside or make friends with neighborhood children. Thus, when newly arrived Solagueños had the means to move out, many opted not to settle in South Central and gravitated toward the neighborhoods of Koreatown and Mid-City, which they deemed less dangerous. A few families, like my own, remained in South Central and its surrounding neighborhoods.

Guillermo, a 26-year-old member of the second generation, reflected on his parents' decision to settle in Mid-City, a neighborhood adjacent to Koreatown:

They didn't know better, you know? They didn't know where we moved, you know? Like back then, you didn't have Google to see what neighborhoods were nice ... what neighborhoods were not. There was a lot of gangs, drugs, violence. It was everywhere. Graffiti ... everything was covered up in gang writing. They had just demolished the elementary school so we had a temporary one which was bungalows and it wasn't nothing solid. We didn't have a playground so we used to go play at the park ... the public park across the street from the school, which is where the gangs just hung out. So sometimes when we were out there playing for recess or for lunch, something would happen. There would be drive-bys ... people getting strung out behind the tree or people fighting ... 'cuz it was a public park. So, there was always something going on at that park. At a young age, we were exposed to so much.

Guillermo paints a vivid portrait of his childhood in Mid-City. His account underscores that while scholars and the media have focused on the social ills affecting South Central during this period, the residents of Mid-City Los Angeles, including Solagueños and their children, were also exposed to the marginalization, criminalization, and disinvestment that plague inner-city neighborhoods. As their American-born Solagueño children would eventually discover through their schooling experiences, these conditions were different from those of their White peers living in more affluent parts of the city.

Like many immigrants,[42] Solagueños live economically and socially segregated from other groups. Guillermo remembered the Mid-City neighborhood where his family moved in the late 1980s as a Black community whose demographics shifted with the arrival of Latinx immigrants. During the time I conducted this research, the demographics of Mid-City reflected a large Latinx and Black population.[43] During his childhood in the early 1990s, as Guillermo describes in the statement that follows, Mid-City was mostly inhabited by Latinx immigrants and their children:

I didn't know what an immigrant was at that time. All our parents were immigrants. It was something normal. No one said, "My dad's from Philadelphia ... from Missouri" or something. You would hear, "My parents are from somewhere in Latin America." It was like that in elementary and middle school. It wasn't 'til I got to high school ... I went to a very diverse school ... that I had my first interaction with White people 'cuz I hadn't been around them my whole life.

Having grown up in a Latinx immigrant neighborhood, Guillermo did not grow up understanding that a person could inhabit an "immigrant" identity. In an immigrant enclave, such an identity was a given and thus unmarked. As a teenager, Guillermo learned that some of his schoolmates' parents were actually born and grew up in other American states rather than in other countries. Guillermo's experience demonstrates the severity of residential segregation and the containment of marginalized communities within a city that has long been lauded for its diversity.

Furthermore, as someone immersed in an immigrant enclave, Guillermo experienced diversity as the opposite of what is usually thought to be diverse—that is, for him it was a space that includes Whites rather than a space that includes people of non-White background. This realization would lead him to learn not only about the existence of the so-called native-born population of the United States, but that nascency, race, and residential location afforded Angelenos different opportunities:

> I realized their English was better. You could notice it. They were smarter at things because obviously they had the better education because they lived on the better side of town ... that's when I knew that I'm different. My English sounds different than theirs. ... That's also when I learned about privilege because my school was on the Westside. ... I would get the school bus and travel from my neighborhood to the Westside. With all that traveling I realized, "Oh look where I live and look where I go to school. It's real different." For the White kids, that was their home school.

Attending a school on the Westside of Los Angeles made Guillermo aware of the disparities between his education and neighborhood and that of his White peers who lived on the Westside. His statement underscores the structural racism embedded in the educational system, especially the low-resource public schools the children of immigrants are placed into as a result of residential segregation.[44] Guillermo's bus ride to school highlighted the differences between neighborhoods in which non-Whites and Whites reside, as well as the disparities between the education youth receive in different neighborhoods. While Mid-City may have seemed like a safer alternative to residing in South Central Los Angeles, it was a non-White and majority Latinx neighborhood and so the inequities Solagueños encountered in their original neighborhood persisted. Guillermo's experience echoes the stories of other Oaxacan and Latinx youth whose exposure to predominantly White schools made them aware that race, class, geography, and power inform their life experiences.[45]

Other Solagueño youth did not have to travel outside of their neighborhoods to become conscious of the disparities between themselves and the children of White Americans. Mateo, a 19-year-old member of the second generation, attended an elite private high school a few blocks away from his home in Koreatown. While Whites account for less than 10 percent of the population of Koreatown, Mateo's high school had a predominantly White student body. The contradictory demographics in the school's student body are a result of the school's establishment in the early twentieth century, prior to the area becoming an immigrant enclave. This was an era marked by the consolidation of power in the city among White elites, in which they not only codified where industry was allowed through zoning laws, but also the areas in which people of color were allowed to buy homes.[46] Mateo noticed differences between himself and his peers, particularly in terms of their upbringing:

> It's just everything's different for them and for us. ... Sometimes I hear them and they're like, "Oh my parents just bought me this thing." "Oh I'm getting a car." I mean, I see the parking lot of my high school and it's just like a bunch of nice cars.

While his neighborhood has been marked by the past racial regimes and ongoing colonialities, for Mateo, the differences between him and his private school peers manifested in the material things their parents were able to afford. Differences in Mateo's and his White peers' lifestyles were even more salient as wealthy White students traveled from their homes in more affluent parts of the city and flaunted their lavish styles in inner-city Los Angeles, safely removed from the structural racism Solagueños endured in their everyday lives. While Mateo and his schoolmates may be unaware of it, Los Angeles was designed to shield Whites from these experiences.

The neighborhoods Solagueños moved into upon arriving in Los Angeles marked their children's childhoods even as they tried to mitigate their experiences by relocating to "safer" neighborhoods. While

Mateo and Guillermo commented on the economic disparities between themselves and their White peers at their schools, neighborhood gangs loomed over the lives of Solagueños and their children. Indeed, moving away from "cholos," or Latinx gang members, was one of the main reasons many Solagueños moved out of South Central Los Angeles. Still, the children of Solagueño immigrants inevitably grew up around gang life as residents of inner-city neighborhoods in Los Angeles, which has been labeled the epicenter of the American gang problem.[47] Scholars posit that youth exposure to drugs, gangs, and crime in inner-city neighborhoods could present an obstacle to their integration into American society.[48] Youth who have been exposed to these aspects of the inner city are more likely to drop out of school and less likely to experience economic upward mobility.[49] The children of low-income undocumented immigrants, in particular, are more likely to live in neighborhoods and attend schools where they are disproportionately exposed to youth involved in gangs and intergroup violence.[50]

The prevalence of gangs came up during interviews with youth, who often portrayed Solaga as a safe place compared to their neighborhoods in Los Angeles, and their eventual involvement in the Solagueño youth band as an escape from their potential involvement in gangs. Guillermo, whom I mentioned earlier, recalled his childhood in Mid-City:

> When I was in elementary school, which was a block away from where I live, there was shootings. This whole thing was like Mid-City gang. They were everywhere. It was crazy! There were shootings here. There were shootings there. Everywhere!

Guillermo also remembered his school would often go on lockdown when there were shootings in the neighborhood. Guillermo's elementary and high school experience demonstrates the different school environments in which Solagueño children grow up, including one where neighborhood shootings are commonplace and another in which they are not even mentioned.

Sam, a 23-year-old member of the second generation, also shared that his neighborhood of Mid-City was home to *La Mara Salvatrucha* and Playboy Gangster Crips:

That was what it was known for back in the day. Those were the gangs that really beefed it. As kids, we would grow up being careful trying not to get involved in that just in case there was a shooting. Just throw yourself down. You know? It was a little bit scary.

In Sam's and Guillermo's cases it seems that there were not direct experiences with gangs but that an acute awareness of potential shootings in their neighborhoods was vital for Solagueño youth. While the neighborhoods of South Central, Koreatown, and Mid-City might have left Solagueño youth vulnerable to gang activity and other dangerous aspects of inner-city life, living in Koreatown and Mid-City also meant that they were surrounded by other Oaxacan immigrants.

Guillermo, Mateo, and Sam's childhood experiences demonstrate how the neighborhoods Solagueños moved into upon arriving in Los Angeles left an impression on their children, but immigrants and their children also leave impressions on the communities in which they reside.[51] As Matias pointed toward in the beginning of the chapter, Oaxacans' strong presence in Koreatown is evident in the number of Oaxacan children in local schools. They represent a demographic shift and add to the cultural diversity of the city. Indeed, Koreatown has become synonomous with Oaxacans. Los Angeles city council member Gil Cedillo pointed toward Koreatown's association with Oaxacans in an audio recording leaked in 2022. In the recording, city council president Nury Martinez comments that she sees "a lot of little short dark people" in Koreatown, to which Cedillo responds, "Yeah, *puro* Oaxacans. *Puro* Oaxacan Koreans."[52] In mocking the physical characteristics associated with Indigenous Oaxacans, as well as their concentration in a Korean ethnic enclave, Cedillo's and Martinez's remarks draw attention to the striking Oaxacan presence in this neighborhood, as well as racial hierarchies within the Latinx community.

The Children of Solagueños in Multiethnic Los Angeles

Just as Angeleno territory is inscribed with the layered experience of Spanish, Mexican, and Anglo colonization, so too are the racialized experiences of Solagueños and their children. Scholars posit that migration leads some immigrants to experience racial prejudice they may not have been subject to in their home countries, since they may become targets and victims of discrimination after moving to the United States.[53] Nevertheless, some immigrants—including those with Indigenous origins—are targets of racial discrimination in their home countries and upon emigrating to the United States.[54] These layered experiences of exclusion stem from White supremacist racial hiearchies that privilege Euro-descendants as the new "natives" and the group most entitled to rights.[55] Under Spanish rule, these beliefs were predicated on the false notion of the inherent inferiority of Native peoples and their culture to that of Spaniards and later Mexican Californios. The *casta* system, which enforced this racial hierarchy, was dissolved when Mexico got its independence from Spain. Still, racial inequality persisted, this time predicated on the alleged innate delinquency of Indigenous and Black peoples.[56]

Upon assuming power in the Los Angeles basin, Anglos instituted their own racial hierarchies that placed them in a position superior to Mexican Californios and ensured that the racial geographies of the city reflected and protected these divisions.[57] In the present day, non-Indigenous Latinx immigrants and their descendants may experience Anglo domination as the most salient form of oppression; hence the emphasis by some migration scholars on the novelty of discrimination for some immigrant groups. However, Indigenous Latinxs' racialized experiences reflect enduring Spanish, Mexican, and Anglo colonialities in their ancestral homelands and in their new home. Thus, for diasporic Solagueños, exclusion and discrimination sometimes comes from within the Latinx community, a pan-ethnic group they are a part of based on a shared language, religion, and natal attachments to places that were once part of the Spanish empire.[58] Because racialized experiences of discrimination in Los Angeles are a result of multiple colonialities and are thus layered, what some diasporic Solagueños identify as an assault on their Indigenous identity, others may attribute to their legal status. Still, all of these experiences inform how Solagueño youth regard themselves and the relationships they have to their ancestral homeland.

Anglo Discrimination

Diasporic Solagueño youth experience prejudice from mainstream American society at an interpersonal level and through political rhetoric. Latinxs have been portrayed in public discourse as "'alien-citizens,' perpetual foreigners with divided allegiances despite being U.S. citizens by birth, even after many generations."[59] Prejudice toward Solagueños on the basis of their national origin may stem from the suspicion that Mexicans are incapable or unwilling to integrate into American society.[60] Guillermo, who was born in Los Angeles, identifies as "Mexican." This identity is both ascribed and self-imposed. Guillermo spoke of being the only person with Mexican origins in his classes at a college on the East Coast, where he was sometimes called a "spic," a racial slur he had not encountered on the West Coast. For Guillermo, this experience underscored the reality that he did not fit the American ideal:

> If a White person sees me walking down the street, they aren't gonna say, "There goes a fellow American. That's a Mexican." You know? I'm not accepted by Americans, but at least I have my identity. It's still something. I might not be accepted by mainstream society, but I'm still someone.

In the scenario Guillermo constructed, a "White" person becomes synonymous with "American." This conflation reflects the reality that in the United States, "real" Americans, that is, those whose claims to an American identity go unchallenged, are White. Although an American citizen by birth, his ethnic identity and his position in the racial hierarchy of the United States leaves Guillermo outside of the American imaginary.[61] Nevertheless, this experience is mediated by his Mexican identity. Having a strong sense of identity is important because if individuals fail to secure an identity, they face identity confusion, which includes a lack of clarity about who they are and what their role in life is.[62] For Guillermo, his Mexican identity provides him with the sense of humanity that his rejection from the American mainstream would deprive him of. Guillermo's feelings of rejection from American society are informed by his interactions with Anglo Americans, as well as his experiences in White spaces, including his high school and college. For other Solagueños, this rejection is a result of Anglo-imposed legal regimes that deem select individuals as worthy of American citizenship.

Most diasporic youths I spoke to were born in the United States; still, as Guillermo's experience suggests, being born in the United States does not ensure inclusion in American society. Undocumented individuals who arrived as children grow up and are educated in the United States with the same upbringing and aspirations as their U.S.-born peers.[63] However, legal status becomes more salient once undocumented youth come of age and find that their legal status prevents them from fulfilling these aspirations.[64] Eduardo was born in Oaxaca and brought to the United States as a child. He shared the difficulties he, his parents, and his brother experienced as undocumented immigrants. This included not having a Social Security number, which in the 1990s meant both he and his family had limited employment opportunities. When asked about his identity, Eduardo expressed uncertainty: "As an immigrant, you feel unwanted in this country and then you're like, so where am I from? Am I from Solaga? Am I from Mexico? Am I from Oaxaca? Where am I wanted?" Eduardo's legal status left him in limbo with no clear understanding of where or *if* he belonged (or was even wanted) on either side of the U.S.-Mexico border. As Eduardo's statement demonstrates, his uncertainty included his native Oaxaca, which one might assume he would have a connection with as his birthplace. Nevertheless, immigrants who migrated as children may not remember their country of origin and they inevitably develop an attachment to the United States. Their American upbringing makes many members of the 1.5 generation de facto aliens in their country of citizenship.[65] This pertains to Eduardo, who is more familiar with American culture than the culture of Mexico, his country of citizenship.

While the United States prides itself on being a nation of immigrants, these immigrants have been separated into "virtuous others," usually reserved for European immigrants, and "undesirable exogenous others," that is, racialized immigrants.[66] As the descendants of Mexican nationals, diasporic Solagueño children and youth fall under the "undesirable exogenous others" category and thus are deemed unworthy of American citizenship even when this status is the legal birthright of U.S.-born Solagueños. While American citizenship may not shield them from racial prejudice toward Mexicans, as I demonstrate in Chapter 3, Solagueños transform American citizenship, particularly the ability to move freely across borders, into a collective resource that the Solagueño community can mobilize to remain connected to their homeland.

Latinx Discrimination

The children of Indigenous immigrants are also privy to rejection from non-Indigenous Latinx immigrants in the United States whom they encounter at school and in their neighborhoods.[67] Solagueños' Indigenous background differentiates them from many of the *mestizo* members of the Latinx community, who are of mixed Spanish and Indigenous ancestry. Solagueño youth in Los Angeles may be singled out by their Latinx and Mexican peers as a result of their physical features. Miguel, an 18-year-old second-generation Solagueño, remarked: "Sometimes Mexicans stereotype Oaxacans. They're like short ... brown. They don't really ask you, but they see Oaxacans as small, short, brown." While Oaxacans are part of and, as Guillermo earlier attested, see themselves as part of the Mexican population, Miguel's statement demonstrates how Oaxacans' Indigenous background sets them apart from *mestizo* Mexican immigrants. As Miguel pointed out, Mexicans do not even have to ask people they may suspect to be Oaxacans if they are in fact Oaxacan. They are able to determine an Indigenous person's race based on their phenotype or the physical characteristics associated with people from Oaxaca, which include being short in stature and having darker skin tones than their *mestizo* counterparts. On their own, these descriptors may be harmless. However, some *mestizo* youth may express prejudice toward Indigenous children and youth as a result of their phenotype.

Rebecca, a 23-year-old member of the 1.5 generation, described how her high school peers held negative attitudes about her Indigenous Oaxacan origin:

> In high school, I think that's pretty much when you find yourself. I remember my friends used to be like, "Oh, Oaxaquita! Oh, you're from Oaxaca! You're a little Indian. Oh, this and that."

"Oaxaquita" is a derogatory term used to describe someone with origins in the predominantly Indigenous state of Oaxaca.[68] Pejorative descriptors like "Oaxaquita" and "little Indian" are meant to and indeed do instill a sense of shame among Indigenous children and youth about their Indigenous identity, culture, and language. I pressed Rebecca on how her classmates determined who was a "Oaxaquita." She replied, "They would say, 'Si son chaparros, prietos, y feos, son de Oaxaca.'"

Among Rebecca's peers, being "short, dark, and ugly" signaled that youth were from Oaxaca. Not fitting this description saved some Indigenous youth from the discrimination faced by their peers who fit the racial descriptor. Luna is a 20-year-old member of the second generation, born to a Mexico City–born Solagueña and a *mestizo*. Luna has a lighter complexion than many of her Solagueño cousins. Although Luna took pride in her Solagueño origin and often defended her Oaxacan friends, people seemed to care less because of her light complexion. Luna's ability to pass as a *mestiza*—with her light skin and green eyes—shows that the animosity Oaxacans endure stems from the racialized characteristics of being "short" and "dark" Indians, phenotypic differences that may distinguish them from the children of Latinx immigrants with *mestizo* origins. *Mestizo* Mexicans and Latinxs leave aspects of their *mestizo* privilege when they migrate to the United States and become racialized minorities and cast as "illegals."[69] However, *mestizo* Latinxs and their children continue to rely on the racial hierarchies Europeans instituted to subjugate Native and Afro-descendant peoples. These racial hiearchies privilege European phenotypes and deem Indigenous and Afro-descendant traits as "ugly" or unattractive. Rebecca's and Luna's experiences with *mestizo* youth indicate that negative connotations associated with people of Indigenous origin carry over to the United States, where some *mestizo* immigrants and their children continue to discriminate against people of Indigenous origin because of their racial background.[70]

Notably, the Solagueño youth who experienced discrimination from their Latinx peers grew up in Mid-City and Koreatown, areas with large Latinx populations. My upbringing in South Central in a predominantly Black Catholic school shielded me from the anti-Indigenous prejudice my Solagueño peers experienced in other parts of the city. As I was one of two Mexican-origin children at the school, my classmates may not have known where to place me within an American racial hierarchy that privileges whiteness and relegates Black Americans to the bottom of the racial order. In the fourth grade, there was one instance in which a classmate made a prejudicial remark about me being "Mexican." However, my Indigenous background was not something my peers picked up on or even knew was something to be ridiculed. While my neighborhood is commonly regarded as a dangerous place, for me, South Central was a safe space in which I could develop and embrace my Indigenous identities.

Social and racial conditions in the neighborhoods the children of Solagueño immigrants grew up in marked their childhoods and set up the conditions that would lead many of these individuals to be active in the traditions of their parents' hometown. The need for a safe alternative to life in their inner-city neighborhoods led some parents to encourage their children's participation in the Solagueño youth band. For some, involvement in the band allowed them to mediate the experiences of discrimination they experienced at the hands of some members of the *mestizo* population. For others, participation in the band allowed them to mediate their negative experiences with members of the White population. Whether a result of Anglo or *mestizo* domination, Solagueño youth were able to develop a positive relationship with aspects of themselves and their identities that others suggested they should hate.

Instrumentalizing Resistance

While Spanish efforts to evangelize Native peoples took on various forms across Spanish America, their common goal was to eradicate Indigenous religions and cultural teachings in favor of that of Europeans. In what became California, this was done through the Franciscan mission system. In Mexico, where evangelization was the charge of the Dominican religious order, patron saint celebrations were instituted as a tool of colonial domination that appropriated Indigenous rituals, dances, and music and made them part of Catholic celebrations. Music was integral to Dominican conversion efforts in newly established parishes in the town Spanish colonizers named Antequera, present-day Oaxaca City, as evidenced by colonial records documenting the demand for musical instruments to be used in Catholic Mass.[71] Music continues to be central to Oaxacan communities because, while originally part of a colonial imposition, musical practices have become a concrete manifestation of Indigenous forms of social organization like the *gozona*, the system of reciprocity among townspeople and between Indigenous towns in the region. Diasporic Oaxacans, both those that have migrated to other parts of Mexico and those that have crossed the border into the United States, have taken with them many cultural traditions from their Indigenous communities. Mixtec and Zapotec brass bands have been established in Mexico City, Oaxaca City, the Mexican state of Morelos, and in California.[72] In Los Angeles, Oaxacan brass bands have become a symbol and marker of Oaxacan identity for diasporic youth.[73] Indeed, as Blackwell states, Oaxacan band and dance groups' "practices, performances, fundraising and gatherings create other Indigenous soundscapes and places within Los Angeles."[74] However, Solagueño community life was different prior to the establishment of *Banda Juvenil Solaga USA Oaxaca,* the first Los Angeles–based band to be composed solely of the children of Oaxacan immigrants.

Prior to the formation of the youth brass band, family gatherings allowed Solagueños to come together in intimate settings to celebrate their culture. Eduardo came of age in Los Angeles in the late 1990s. He remembered that Solagueño social events were

> mostly birthday parties between family members but not like *kermeses* or big huge parties. At that time, the only events I can remember are gatherings between family members and at those gatherings it was like a celebration of our culture because of the food, because of the language, because people were speaking *Zapoteco,* because of the music. People would take out their tapes and play it during the party.

Eduardo's account underscores two major differences between the Solagueño events of his youth and those of today: the live music component and the scale of these events. Since the band's inception, what originated as small family gatherings transformed into large fundraisers and "huge parties" for patron saints that all Solagueños and Oaxacans are welcome to attend. As opposed to private events with a limited guest list, these events are now open to the public and thus gather larger crowds. Moreover, instead of the cassette tapes of Eduardo's youth, these events now have live music played by brass bands composed of Oaxacan children and youth trained as musicians in the diaspora. Still, as Eduardo indicated, small social gatherings provided a space in which Solagueños could come together to pay homage to and celebrate their community and culture before the formation of *Banda Juvenil Solaga USA Oaxaca.*

Banda Juvenil Solaga USA Oaxaca was formed by Antonio, a Solagueño immigrant who arrived in Los Angeles in 2001. A trained musician, Antonio pitched the idea of creating a youth village-based band to his *paisanos* by word of mouth. Jaime, a Mexico City–born Solagueño, joined the band as an 11-year-old. He recalled, "I was there the first day they started. ... It was probably like ten of us. It was just an idea." Eventually, fifty children joined the band. "That I know," Jaime continued, "it was the first band that I know with kids that were born here or the majority was born here." This new band was different from previous iterations of Los Angeles–based Oaxacan bands, which were composed of first-generation immigrants. The members of what became *Solaga USA* were the children of Solagueño immigrants: youth who were brought to the United States as children or children who were born in Los Angeles to Solagueño immigrants. While first-generation musicians had to be mindful of work schedules for band practice and performances, children and youths' more flexible schedules afforded them the opportunity to practice during the week and perform at weekend events with more frequency. While *Solaga USA* was the first Oaxacan band to feature solely the children of immigrants, other Los Angeles–based Oaxacan bands soon followed suit. Today, most members of Oaxacan bands in Los Angeles are the children of Oaxacan immigrants.

The large number of recruits demonstrates the Solagueño community's enthusiasm to establish a youth band. Indeed, playing in a Oaxacan brass band was an activity youth could partake in that was uniquely rooted in their ancestral practices. Jaime, who had spent part of his childhood in Solaga, was familiar with the music and was immediately interested in joining the band. He remembered wanting to join the band in Solaga, but feeling that "maybe [he] wasn't good enough to play with them yet." In other Solagueño families, however, recruiting prospective band members became a multi-generational endeavor. Some of the original members of *Solaga USA* were reluctant to join the band. Guillermo described how he was recruited at age 13 to be part of *Solaga USA*:

> Pretty much my dad forced me. I remember him telling me and my sister, "We're forming a Solaga band. We want to form a band and they need young men and women if you want to learn music and be part of a Oaxacan

regional band." My sister was like, "Okay, I'll go!" She liked music. She's always liked music. I liked it too but at that time, I mostly listened to rap like Snoop Dogg and Dre. That's mostly what I listened to ... Tupac ... all that stuff. I wasn't really interested. I was like, "Nah, I'm cool." You know? I used to have a lot of friends where I lived. There was more than a dozen of us that lived in the same building. We used to play and hang out after school. I was on a soccer team and I was mainly doing that and hanging out, so I wasn't really interested. So, my sister went and when she came back she was like, "You should go! You should go!" and I was like "Nah nah" and then the following week came, and it was time to go again and my dad was like, "You should go, Guillermo. You should at least see. You might like it. You never know." I was like, "Nah," and then they convinced me. So that's pretty much how I got forced.

For youth like Guillermo, Oaxacan music did not line up with their lives in the diaspora in terms of their social circles, as well as their musical taste. While his family moved away from the neighborhoods from which Guillermo's favorite rappers drew inspiration, their lyrics more accurately reflected the realities of growing up in inner-city Los Angeles. This music often responded to that violence and vocalized Black youths' understanding that their lot in life was a result of the decimation of social services and police repression in communities of color.[75] Earlier, Guillermo shared how he often witnessed gang violence growing up in his neighborhood of Mid-City. These shootings were so commonplace that Guillermo started to become desensitized to the violence. Participating in the band, Guillermo shared, gave him an alternative to the lifestyle available to him in his neighborhood. He came to see the band as an escape, something to which his neighborhood friends, many of whom were later incarcerated, were not privy.

Guillermo's memories of the time continue to be imbued with the perspective he had as a teenager, particularly the idea that he was forced to join the band. Guillermo's father, himself a musician and the son of a musician, may have seen the formation of the youth band as a unique opportunity for his own children to engage in a multigenerational family tradition. Thus, the opportunity his children now had allowed them to play music from his hometown and this may have led him to pressure them to join this new band, thereby shaping how Guillermo remembers this time. His family's insistence that Guillermo at least experience band rehearsal for himself afforded him the chance to witness the community that the band members and their parents were building and to eventually travel to the home community and perform with his cousins in Solaga's municipal band, as he shares in Chapter 4.

Some parents were also reluctant to have their children participate in the band. Solagueño immigrants understood the time-intensive nature of being a *bi wekuell*, a musician, in their hometown. Being a member of Solaga's municipal band is equivalent to a *cargo* because of the level of commitment musicians invest in these activities. As part of the band, *bi wekuell* perform at community events, including patron saint celebrations and funerals, and travel to surrounding communities for musical exchanges as part of the *gozona*—a practice that allows Solagueños to foster good relations between their community and neighboring communities. Lorena, a 49-year-old Solagueña, remembered that she had been opposed to the idea of her children joining the band, while her husband had actively encouraged his children to participate in the band. Lorena believed being in the band would be too time consuming. Indeed, Jaime, whom I mentioned earlier, remembered that between rehearsals and their performances the band would get together every day of the week. Lorena's oldest son, Josué, was friends with several Solagueño children who joined the band in 2001 and he decided to do so, too. She tried to get Josué to quit, but to no avail.

Later, Lorena's younger children Arturo and Araceli also joined the band. Arturo, 19 years old at the time of the interview, recalled:

> I've been in the band since I was 6 years old. I started off when I was that young, but my brother had been in the band, since he's a couple of years older. So, I was kind of surrounded by that culture since before I wanted [i.e., before I had a choice] so I guess just watching them kind of encouraged me to join and I've been part of it since then.

Arturo recognized the role of growing up surrounded by Oaxacan music. This was a result of accompanying his older brother to practice and eventually to performances. Josué and Arturo's younger sister, Araceli, joined the band when she was 4 years old. Although Josué quit the band once he left for college, Arturo and Araceli stayed. As a result of her children's desire to participate in the Solagueño youth band, Lorena had been involved with the band for more than fifteen years. In this time, Lorena's backyard had become a center for Solagueño social gatherings, particularly those hosted by the Solagueño youth band.

Other youths made the decision to join the band through their involvement in other aspects of Solagueño life in Los Angeles rather than through earlier attempts from their parents to recruit them for the band. Matias, who at the beginning of this chapter declared his high school to be "Home of the Oaxacans," joined *Solaga USA* when he was 9 years old, years after his father attempted to persuade him to join the band by taking him to band practice with his older brothers. Matias recalled, "I didn't want to go to band practice. My dad says once I kicked him in the shin and left crying because I didn't want to do it." Participating in a *danza* made him change his mind about being part of *Solaga USA*. "After joining a *danza* I heard the band and I was like, 'Oh, that sounds fun!' So then I joined." While Arturo attributes his participation in the band to growing up around the band because of his older brother's participation, Matias only grew interested in *Solaga USA* experiencing the music as a dancer. Like Guillermo, Matias, and others, when I was asked to join the band as a pre-teen, it was not something that piqued my interest. At the time, my summer trips to visit my maternal grandmother were how I maintained my connection to Solaga. However, I did bear witness to the change that having a brass band had on my community—with the creation of *Solaga USA*, patron saint celebrations and community events became more frequent. Youths who were part of these bands and the *danzas* that were organized to perform at patron saint festivities became increasingly more important in staging these celebrations.

La escoleta

The creation of *Solaga USA* gave diasporic Solagueños in Los Angeles the opportunity to come together more regularly. For some of the young musicians, participating in the band was not only their first encounter with Oaxacan music but also an opportunity for children and youth to see their parents engage in the communal practices rooted in their ancestral ways of knowing and being in the world. Sara, a U.S.-born Solagueña, recalled her experience joining the band when she was 10 years old:

I was not ... how can I say it? Cultured. Because my parents wouldn't really go to Solaga parties to interact with their *paisanos*. So I mean I didn't know many of the kids that were there when I started. I only knew my close cousins but everything was new. I didn't know how to dance *jarabes*. My parents wouldn't listen to *jarabes* at home so it was new to me. ... The music was different. It was exciting because it was like happy music to me and I enjoyed it and I learned a lot about Oaxaca and the culture and then I went to Solaga and that was fun because I had been to Solaga only once before that time but it was when I was like 5 so I didn't remember what it was like.

Sara's participation in the band served as her introduction to Solagueño and Oaxacan culture, an aspect of her identity she had not experienced in her home. The band allowed her and her family to *convivir*, or engage with, their *paisanos* beyond their immediate relatives. Sara notes not only the feeling of happiness *jarabes* invoked within her, but that learning how to dance *jarabes* made her more "cultured." Her remark shows the importance of music and dance as a form of embodied knowledge among Zapotec peoples.[76] López Oro identifies this form of knowledge as ancestral memory and notes how dancing and drumming are an embodied archive of Garifuna epistemologies.[77] Music and dance connects Sara and other diasporic Solagueños to our *pueblo* both as a people and as a place. The feeling of happiness Sara got from playing and learning how to dance *jarabes* shows how she began to engage *el goce comunal* or the feeling of communal joy community members feel from their contribution to and participation in communal life. Sara's involvement in the band allowed her to engage in Indigenous practices of belonging as a *bi wekuell* and afforded her the opportunity to return to her ancestral homeland in this capacity, an experience I discuss in Chapter 3. As a *bi wekuell*, she was also able to witness how band parents practiced *comunalidad*.

The first generation of *Solaga USA* practiced in the garages and backyards of Solagueño homes. Noise complaints led band parents to look for a practice space where there would not be such issues. Their search led them to an apartment building in the Adams-Normandie neighborhood of Los Angeles, close to the Mid-City and Koreatown neighborhoods where most Solagueños live. There, they were able to rent a single-room occupancy apartment for their children to practice and where the band still rehearsed at the time of this research. *Solaga USA*'s rehearsal space became known as *la escoleta,* the same name for the rehearsal space for Solaga's municipal band in the hometown. The band parents I spoke to recalled paying $20 a month for their child to participate in the band. Former band members could not recall how much it cost for them to participate in the band; they were children, they reminded me. This money was used to pay Antonio, the music teacher, and to cover the monthly rent for the rehearsal space. Sara noted that the parents "would also help each other. They would do *kermeses* [fundraisers], food sales, so we could collect money." Importantly, Sara highlights the *gozona* or mutual aid among Solagueños. Her recollection of the fundraisers parents hosted to cover *Solaga USA*'s expenses highlights not only the reciprocity among band parents but also the communal nature of this project. Through their unremunerated communal labor, band parents worked together so that their children could participate in the band. In comparing the $50 a month she thought her parents paid to the $100 an hour she estimated private lessons are, she highlights the power of communal life. *Solaga USA* provided children and youth with access to affordable and quality musical training they likely would not have been able to receive outside of this setting. As Matias stated earlier, this transformed how Oaxacans are imagined within Los Angeles.

Band-related expenses, Sara noted, were also offset by money the band raised by playing private events. Since its inception, the Los Angeles-based Solagueño youth band has maintained an active profile. Oaxacan brass bands are indispensable to patron saint festivities, weddings, and funerals as these rituals require musical accompaniment. *Solaga USA*'s performance schedule revolves around the aforementioned events, as well as *bailes* (dances), *kermeses, quinceañeras,* and other milestone celebrations. As Oaxacans have adopted traditions in diaspora,[78] they have incorporated their musical practices into these traditions. The *baile sorpresas* for Solagueño *quinceañeras,* for example, are now usually a *jarabe* rather than, or in addition to, a choreographed dance to popular Latinx music. As a result of the large Serrano community in Los Angeles, there are several events every weekend, which keeps *Solaga USA* busy.

These events are staged in dance halls, warehouses, and parking lots that are rented for these celebrations, as well as in community members' backyards. While the band's steering committee organizes celebrations in honor of *La Virgen del Carmen* and *San Andrés,* Solaga's two major patron saints, some Solagueño families host celebrations in honor of other saints venerated in the community. These families hire the Solagueño youth band or other Los Angeles–based bands to perform at their events. These celebrations have had to be refashioned to fit the confines of Solagueño life in Los Angeles and, more pragmatically, the confines of the spaces let out for these celebrations. Solagueños, especially those that are unable to return to Solaga because of their unauthorized status, make do with *fiestas* in Los Angeles. However, diasporic Solagueños who have experienced *fiestas* in Solaga and Los Angeles note the differences between these celebrations. Sara notes:

> It's different. So, it's the city. Right? Everyone's there just for ... just for a short period of time and most of the time it's like you can feel like ... it's nice but you can also feel some kind of chaos at the same time 'cuz there's so much going around but it isn't the same feeling as if you were in the *pueblo.* ... The places are smaller, you have people eating. You have people walking around. It doesn't feel the same.

Like Perla in the previous chapter, Sara highlights the importance of experiencing these celebrations in the communal territory. She notes how the reconfiguration of key aspects of Solagueño festivities that are usually spread out across our hometown during multiple days into a smaller setting and a shorter period of time can feel chaotic. Her perspective is informed by her ability to cross the border and witness these celebrations in our ancestral homeland. The communal spaces *Solaga USA* has been able to create have, nevertheless, been critical for Sara and other diasporic Solagueños' identity formation and for the Solagueño community across borders.

Conclusion

What began as a small Zapotec town's effort to inculcate an appreciation for their hometown's cultural practices transformed diasporic life for Solagueños, their children, and other Oaxacans living in Los Angeles. Private social gatherings were magnified to partially reflect the scale of patron saint celebrations in Solagueños' homeland. Yet these celebrations had to be refashioned to fit the confines of Solagueño life in Los Angeles and, more pragmatically, the confines of the dilapidated party halls, warehouses, and backyards let out for these celebrations. The Solagueño youth band and the events at which they performed created spaces in which Indigenous immigrants could transmit an appreciation for their culture and community values to their children away from their homeland.

Rebecca, whom I mentioned earlier, attributed the pride she feels in her Indigenous background to her time in *Solaga USA*:

> I don't know if I would have been as close to my culture as I am if I hadn't joined the band. I have to give credit to the band. I liked it ... playing *sones y jarabes* from the region. I love dancing *jarabes*. All the traditions they have here [Solaga], we have there [Los Angeles]. If they hold the Virgen del Carmen celebration [in Solaga], we hold the celebration there [in Los Angeles] too.

Despite the anti-Indigenous prejudice Rebecca experienced at the hands of her Latinx peers, Rebecca's participation in the Solagueño youth band allowed her to be in touch with her culture and gain an appreciation for Solagueño music and dance. Children and youth's retention of Solagueño culture is particularly important in the context of Los Angeles, where Solagueño youth face anti-Indigenous discrimination from *within* the Latinx population, as well as anti-Mexican and anti-Latinx discrimination from the American mainstream. The pride Solagueño youth experience as part of *Banda Juvenil Solaga USA* allows them to maintain a positive sense of self in the face of prejudice from the groups they encounter in the United States.

The formation of the youth band represented an outlet for Solagueño youth through which they could stay connected to their parents' culture and also create strong relationships among the Oaxacan community in L.A., since Solagueños began to celebrate their patron saints away from their hometown more frequently than before the youth band existed. As Matias pointed out, the concentration of Oaxacan immigrants in Los Angeles's Koreatown allows their children to grow up among other Oaxacan youth. For Solagueño youth, growing up in inner-city neighborhoods may make them subject to poor schooling and expose youth to gang violence. However, youth have found comfort living in close proximity to other Oaxacans. Having a viable Oaxacan community enables immigrant youth and adults to maintain social connections to cultural beliefs and practices shared by Solagueños in both Los Angeles and Solaga. The cultural presence of Oaxacans in Los Angeles is evident on Pico Boulevard, a street that runs from the city of Santa Monica to Downtown Los Angeles. The Mid-City and Koreatown sections of this street are lined with Oaxacan businesses, spanning ice cream shops, hardware stores, and restaurants. During the summer, Oaxacans parade along Pico Boulevard as part of a *convite tradicional*, a procession in which village-based bands play traditional music as Oaxacan immigrants and their children walk and dance alongside them.

As a result of their participation in their Indigenous community life, disaporic Solagueño youth have been able to transform Los Angeles from a site where they may experience layered forms of exclusion to what Matias terms "Home of the Oaxacans." Within the span of fifteen years, Oaxacan brass bands allowed Solagueños and other Indigenous Oaxacans to foster a strong sense of community pride. While Oaxacans continue to be ostracized by Latinxs because of their Indigenous origins, playing in the village-based band, performing traditional dances, or attending patron saint festivities mediates Solagueño youth experiences of discrimination in the United States by fostering a strong sense of ethnic pride in spite of discrimination from some members of the *mestizo* Latinx population. For displaced peoples, feeling at "home" is more radical when read against the multiple forms of exclusion that remind Oaxacans, as Eduardo put it, that they are unwanted.

THREE

Returning to the Land of the Fallen Leaves

I MET FELIX, THEN 30 years old, at his friend's internet café a few days after Solaga's *Virgen del Carmen fiesta* concluded in the summer of 2016. Having spent the last week playing as part of Solaga's municipal band, Felix now had more time to relax. Most visitors had left and locals were back at their usual haunts. While I was originally there to interview Alfonso, the owner of the internet café, he encouraged me to interview Felix, while Alfonso tended to his customers. Felix agreed to the interview and we moved to the steps leading down to the café to chat. During the course of the interview, I asked Felix, who was born and raised in Solaga, why he thought Solagueños returned to their hometown for patron saint festivities. He posited that Solagueño immigrants returned to the hometown because *"extrañan a su tierra"*—they miss their homeland. His response alludes to Indigenous peoples' relationship to land and to Indigenous Oaxacans' relationship to their *pueblos*, particularly their strong identification with their community of origin and its people.[1] Not yearning or acting on a longing for place may be seen as a rejection of their community identity. "People that do not return," Felix continued, "well, I feel like they do not feel like they are from here. They deny their identity ... the place where they were born, and that's why they don't want to return."

Because place and identity are so intertwined for Solagueños, a refusal to return when one is able to can be considered a rejection of Solagueño identity. Felix's response highlights the transborder dynamics within his own family. While his aunts and uncles migrated to the United States without authorization, they have since adjusted their legal status and are now able to travel to Solaga without trepidation. His remarks are thus a commentary on community members who are able to return to the home community but decide against it. Legal status, however, prevents many undocumented Solagueños from returning to their homeland. The importance Solagueños place on the home community necessitates that their U.S.-born children experience the place where their parents were born and raised. For undocumented Solagueños this often means sending their children to the home community under the care of flight attendants as unaccompanied minors or with community members who are American citizens by birth or who have been able to adjust their status. In doing so, Solagueños mobilize settler-created legal identities to maintain connections with their *pueblo*.

In this chapter, I argue that Solagueño immigrants embark on return trips with their children or encourage them to visit their hometown to allow them to *convivir* with their *pueblo*. In this case, *pueblo* refers to both Solaga and its people. I characterize *convivencia* as the practice of living and engaging with people and place through which Indigenous peoples form and cultivate bonds with their *pueblo* and come to belong to their community.[2] Through *convivencia* in the ancestral homeland, diasporic children and youth are able to experience their Indigenous culture and homeland in the flesh. The appreciation they gain for their *pueblo* and the communal joy they may experience through *fiestas* in the *pueblo* may encourage them to build and maintain relations with Solaga and its people into adulthood. Globalization and neoliberal policies have displaced thousands of Indigenous peoples from their communities of origin and forced them to migrate to the U.S. for a chance at survival.[3] In doing so, these forces have brought about obstacles for *convivencia* in the ancestral homeland. For Solagueños and other Indigenous Oaxacans whose community membership hinges on their active participation in community life, the inability to travel across borders due to legal status may disrupt opportunities for *convivencia* that would be experienced through quotidian life, while fulfilling *cargos*,[4] and by participating in patron saint celebrations in the hometown. Since Solagueños come from a society where individuals represent a larger set of relations, Solagueños are able to *convivir* with their *pueblo* through their children despite being physically absent from the community. Being socialized in the United States, however, creates cultural differences and potential obstacles to *convivencia* for children and youth in the diaspora. Still, the relationships diasporic children and youth build with and in Solaga encourages them to return to their homeland and inevitably influences diasporic community life in Los Angeles, as I discuss in Chapter 4.

Refusing Borders

The experiences of diasporic children and youth with Solaga vary on multiple axes, including their and their parents' immigration status, as well their participation in community life as part of the Solagueño diaspora. Living in a mixed-status family, or a family composed of members with different legal statuses, is not an uncommon experience among Solagueños in Los Angeles. The racial, social, and economic marginalization of Indigenous peoples in Mexico coupled with increasingly restrictive U.S. immigration policies make it almost impossible for Indigenous immigrants to migrate to the U.S. with authorization.[5] With little opportunity to migrate with authorization, Solagueños are forced to migrate clandestinely. Kevin's parents migrated to the United States in the early 1980s, leaving two of their children with their grandparents in Solaga. Under the Immigration Reform and Control Act of 1986, Kevin's parents were eligible for legalization but did not apply.[6] Since they planned to return to Solaga, they considered adjusting their status as a futile and expensive endeavor.

In the intervening years, however, Kevin and two more siblings were born, which fundamentally changed their parents' plans. With five children living in two separate countries, Kevin's parents may have felt more pressure to provide for all of their children,[7] something that would be made more difficult without their American wages. Still, they maintained a strong relationship with their hometown, including through their children's participation the Los Angeles–based youth band, *Banda Juvenil Solaga USA Oaxaca*. Kevin's mother even returned with her U.S.-born children on a trip the band took to Solaga. Knowing that she might not be able to cross back into the United States, the family agreed that Kevin, the youngest child, would stay with his mother in Solaga. As he shared his family's story, he reflected on the very real possibility that he might have grown up in the hometown had his mother been apprehended at the border. Since then, Kevin's family has developed different strategies to remain connected to their *pueblo*, including sending Kevin to Solaga as an unaccompanied minor.

When discussing his return trips to Solaga, Kevin reflected on his privilege as an American citizen, as well as the very real implications legal status continues to have on his family's life:

> Now that I'm older, I'm able to appreciate visiting Solaga more. To be able to go back as I please. Sometimes I feel bad *because of me* my parents can't go back. They can't really go back without fearing what's going to happen to their sons. It makes me appreciate it more. My mom's not able to see her mom. How can you not miss your mom? What is that? Why is it like that?[8]

Kevin's situation is emblematic of many children of undocumented Solagueño immigrants. As American citizens, they can travel across the U.S.-Mexico border for return visits to their parents' hometown of San Andrés Solaga with ease, while their parents must remain in Los Angeles for fear of not being able to return to the United States. His remarks demonstrate that from a young age the children of undocumented Solagueños are cognizant of their parents' predicament: traveling to their hometown not only means possible separation from their children in the U.S., it also means actual family separation from parents and relatives living in Solaga. Diasporic Solagueño youth like Kevin may internalize the U.S. laws and policies that separate undocumented people and their loved ones and blame themselves for their parents' continued unauthorized presence in the U.S.

Part of the injurious consequences of legal violence, or how immigration laws directly and indirectly punish undocumented immigrants for being in the U.S. without authorization, are the normalization, internalization, and legitimation of inequality and hierarchy among "dominated social groups who then accept these categories and evaluate their conditions through these frames and think of their predicament as normal, thus perpetuating unequal social structures."[9] Laura Enriquez and San Juanita García extend the concept of legal violence to the children and descendants of Mexican and Latinx immigrants, who they argue continue to be "punished" or stigmatized for their, their parents', or their co-nationals' actual or assumed unauthorized entry into the United States.[10] For instance, Kevin blaming himself for his parents' inability to return to their hometown demonstrates how legal violence affects the children of immigrants. While immigrants may blame themselves for not being able to provide for or protect their children due to their legal status, their children may also hold themselves responsible for their parents' continued unauthorized presence in the U.S. In Kevin's mind, if it were not for their U.S.-born children, his parents could return to Mexico. However, he also questions the legal policies that separate his mother from her family in Solaga. In questioning the logic of immigration laws, Kevin reminds us that these legal constructs privilege some individuals, while others find it impossible to gain legal entry into the United States and must resort to clandestine migration. With undocumented Solagueños unable to risk their families' livelihoods in the U.S. and Mexico, maintaining kinship across borders falls to diasporic children and youth whose birthright citizenship allows them to move across borders to *convivir* in their ancestral homeland. Although having children may dissuade many immigrants from permanently returning to their home country,[11] as is the case with Kevin's family, Indigenous children also help connect immigrants to their families in their hometowns.[12] Through their transborder movement, diasporic Indigenous children and youth are able to maintain community, ritual, and familial connections with their ancestral homeland. Their American citizenship—a settler-created status—affords them the mobility denied to their undocumented parents. As Valentina later suggests, undocumented parents encourage their children to make use of their citizenship to travel to their hometown.

Following Mohawk anthropologist Audra Simpson, who conceptualizes refusal as "an option for producing and maintaining alternative structures of thought, politics and traditions away from and in critical relationship to states,"[13] I conceptualize diasporic Solagueño children and youth's transborder movement as an act of refusal or transgression against settler states' attempts to limit Indigenous peoples' movement within and across settler-imposed borders.[14] A settler state's authority to limit Indigenous peoples' movement within a territory, Georgina Clarsen argues, is foundational to settler colonialism, as is "the potential and actual capacities of settlers to roam as autonomous sovereign subjects around the world and across the territories they claim as their own."[15] While the capacity of Indigenous Latinx immigrants to be settlers continues to be in question,[16] American citizenship undoubtedly affords U.S. citizen Solagueños privileges originally intended for White settlers, including the right to citizenship and ability to move freely across borders. Consequently, birthright citizenship has been and continues to be challenged when bestowed on non-White citizens born on U.S. territory.[17] Rather than allow their children to experience a de facto undocumented status, diasporic Solagueños refuse U.S. attempts to limit their mobility and their relationship to their homeland. Instead, Solagueños mobilize community members' American citizenship to build and maintain kinship and community across borders.

Solagueños and their children have transformed American citizenship into a collective resource that can be mobilized by community members across settler borders. Through their children, Solagueños are able to practice *convivencia* despite living under settler-created conditions that restrict their movement and attempt to limit their physical engagement with their *pueblo*. Employing autochthonous understandings of the self where children are an extension of their parents and relatives, undocumented Solagueños are also able to *convivir* with their *pueblo*. Return trips, then, also become a way to mediate displacement. In sending or encouraging their children to travel to Solaga, families enable diasporic children and youth to experience the hometown for themselves and their undocumented relatives. Felix believes that parents "instill returning in their children and [their children, in turn,] feel more Solagueño." While return trips among diasporic children and youth may have emerged as a means to circumvent the limits placed on Solagueño mobility, these trips have become critical for identity formation among the Solagueño diaspora as they deepen and strengthen ties to the homeland.

Convivencia

Interviewing diasporic Solagueños and Solagueños in the hometown allowed me to gain perspective on why community members thought diasporic children and youth returned to the hometown. Felix, for example, observed that some U.S.-born Solagueños returned because "their parents bring them with them or encourage them to come" to the community. "Little by little," he added, "the way of life here piques their interest, the *fiesta* … sometimes they want to go walk in the *campo* after the *fiesta* … visit family members." Felix points toward the appeal of *fiestas* and how these draw Solagueños to their homeland and how their children themselves come to revel in *el goce comunal* and are then drawn to come again. *Convivencia* in and with Solaga, then, emerges as one of the reasons for engaging in return trips among children, youth, and community members and as a precursor for partaking in return trips and continued involvement in the community into adulthood.

Familial Convivencia

Through *convivencias familiares* during patron saint celebrations, Urrieta and Martínez's research suggests, multiple generations of a P'urépecha family can gather with their extended relatives living in the hometown and in different parts of Mexico and the United States to socialize.[18] P'urépecha migrants encourage their children to visit their hometown because they believe that to know a place, a person, or a thing means to experience them in the flesh and with one's flesh.[19] These types of experiences are quintessential aspects of *convivencia* that highlight the importance of experiential and embodied knowledges in Indigenous worlds. Thus, while Solagueños have re-created and adapted their way of life and cultural celebrations to their lives in diaspora, they still attach special significance to returning to the hometown for patron saint festivities. Such experiential and embodied knowledges are critical for Indigenous people's understandings of self, people, and place.[20]

The impetus behind Valentina's first return trip was for her to *convivir* with her family members and to experience her parents' hometown. Valentina, who was born in Los Angeles to undocumented Solagueño immigrants, shared: "[My parents] sent me 'cuz they didn't have papers and also because they wanted me to meet my grandparents and my aunt that was still living there along with her younger son. I think they just wanted me to get to know the place. Like to see where they grew up." After this trip, Valentina's mother continued to encourage her to travel to Solaga to visit her grandmother. During our conversation Valentina jokingly summed up her mother's requests as: "go sit your grandma." While sitting with her grandmother may seem mundane, this act takes on more meaning given the fact that Valentina's parents and other undocumented Solagueños cannot share in these everyday moments with family and friends in Solaga. Instead, they have been forced to migrate to the U.S. for their and their community's survival. Still, community members find ways to maintain connections across the U.S.-Mexico border, including mobilizing U.S.-born Solagueños' American citizenship. While such a mobilization of U.S. citizenship may seem like a pragmatic way to circumvent border restrictions, diasporic return trips also allow Indigenous children and youth to *convivir* with family members in the hometown and allow them to build and maintain kinship and community across borders.

Convivencia *with Place*

Return trips also afford diasporic children and youth opportunities to *convivir* with their *pueblo* as a place. Notably, Felix's earlier remark draws a connection between *el campo* and the community's way of life. Many local families continue to work the land as subsistence farmers, growing staple foods for their family's consumption.[21] Most Los Angeles–based Solagueños, on the other hand, work in the service industry in an urban metropolis where they and their children can become alienated from their ancestral way of life. Felix's observation not only acknowledges the differences between Solagueños' way of life in Los Angeles and Solaga, but also why diasporic Solagueños may be drawn to the community and its natural environment.

For Fernando, a 22-year-old second-generation Solagueño, Solaga's allure is that it is the antithesis of Los Angeles:

> Every time I can, I try to go. If I'm having any troubles in the States, I just catch a flight to Solaga and I go. It feels like home. It's just green, like nature. There isn't concrete, just fresh air. It's just so different. You just get lost. You're traveling to an enchanted place and you just get lost.

Here, Fernando's juxtaposition between Solaga and Los Angeles underscores aspects of himself and his relationship to these places. As a U.S.-born

Solagueño, he has the ability to travel to Solaga when he pleases. Indeed, this privilege grants him an escape from his life in the United States. Part of Fernando's "troubles" may come from the way Solagueños are incorporated into the U.S. as laborers, where immigrants and their children often must work multiple jobs to eke out a living. Local Solagueños are not entirely divorced from capitalism. After all, they exist within the settler capitalist state of Mexico, where their way of life continues to be undermined and threatened by capitalist values.[22] The community and Solagueño families also rely on remittances sent by community and family members who make a living from wage labor in the United States. Still, trips to Solaga allow diasporic children and youth a glimpse into their ancestral way of life, one that better recognizes people's worth outside of their wage labor. Diasporic returnees, like Fernando, may associate this different way of life with Solaga's topography. And other diasporic Solagueños may find comfort in the ways in which Solagueños relate to each other in Solaga.

Convivencia *with* Paisanos

Through return trips, Indigenous people in diaspora can live among and engage with community members living in the hometown, as well as those also engaging in return trips. The opportunities for *convivencia* that are part of the festivities in Solaga—where Solagueños living in Mexico City, Oaxaca City, and Los Angeles can come together with locals and people from neighboring communities in celebration of their patron saint *in* their hometown—offer the children of displaced Solagueños a first-hand experience of people in *their* place and ground a displaced people to their community. For children and youth raised outside of their *pueblo*, moreover, *convivencia* in the ancestral homeland allows them build and maintain relations with people and place. While these return trips may last as little as a few days or as long as a few weeks, during their visits diasporic Solagueños are able to tap into genealogical and historical relationships among Solagueños. These relationships often predate individuals and extend to ancestral relationships between family and community members. In other words, *convivencia* that occurred among previous generations of Solagueños fosters a sense of kinship, familiarity, community, and responsibility among living community members and ensures the viability of the community.

While Serranos, people from the communities of the Sierra Juarez of Oaxaca, are intentional about spending time with each other,[23] *convivencia* also emerges in quotidian aspects of communal life, including through social and political organization. This extends to the Serrano diaspora, which is a result of multiple migrations: first from *pueblos* in the Sierra Norte to Oaxaca City and Mexico City, and eventually to the United States. For instance, Gutierrez Nájera and Alonso Ortiz draw a connection between the Zapotec system of reciprocity known as *gwzon* and the ties immigrants from Villa Hidalgo Yalalag in Los Angeles establish through the emotional, financial, and social support they lend community members in times of need, including after the death of a family member.[24] While the support they can provide may vary, Yalaltecos act on a sense of responsibility for their *paisanos*. This sense of responsibility is established through the deceased's and the deceased's family's involvement in the community. The relationships fostered by community members through their participation in these events are what Serranos reap through *convivencia*.

As the aforementioned example demonstrates, despite distance from the hometown, this relationality persists in diaspora. Citlali Fabián grew up Oaxaca City and hails from Yalalag. Her photographic work "grapples with internal migration, intimacy, relationality, and belonging."[25] Fabián's wet collodion photography method, Lourdes Alberto argues, critiques a photographic technique and archive from which Indigenous peoples were excluded. The images Fabián produces would not be possible, Alberto posits, without the "longstanding kinships and intimacies she has maintained with her subjects. Only such deep intimacies make her images possible, precisely because the wet collodion method can require exposure times from twenty seconds to five minutes for the images to be imprinted onto glass. Through the stillness, the photographer and subject must breathe together, maintain eye contact, and stay connected."[26] Fabián's process necessitates an intimacy and sense of relationality made possible through *convivencia*. Indeed, Alberto's interview process entailed familial and communal *convivencia* with Fabián who, like Alberto, is a member of the Yalalteco diaspora. Alberto interviewed Fabián, who is her relative and *paisana*, over a meal and was accompanied by her siblings and their children. Fabián's and Alberto's processes demonstrate how for Serranos in diaspora, *convivencia* entails an engagement with community members that calls on kinship and community ties and extends into cultural and knowledge production. Sitting for a portrait or a research interview, then, become moments for Serranos to relate to each other as kin and *paisanos*.

Convivencia has been integral to my return trips to my parents' hometown of Solaga, as well as my research among Solagueños in Los Angeles and Solaga. Through my return visits to Solaga, I began to see myself and relate to others as Solagueños do. When I was a child, my grandmother advised me, "When people ask you who you are, tell them you are Pacho Arce's granddaughter." She assured me that letting people know who my deceased grandfather was would garner a warm welcome no matter where I went in the Sierra. Importantly, she communicated that for Solagueños, I was not just Daina Sanchez—I was part of a larger set of relations. My grandmother's advice continues to echo in my thoughts when Solagueños and other Serranos inquire into my background. When I tell people I am Pacho Arce's granddaughter, I often hear back, "Your grandfather was my best friend" and immediately feel the warmth of the comradery my grandfather fostered. Even diasporic Solagueño youth bring up my lineage. "My dad says your *abuelito* used to take him hunting," Rebecca, a 1.5-generation Solagueña, told me. These outings meant so much to her father that he related these decades-old memories to his daughter as she did to me when we met. "Your mother wore a dress the color of that bag when she participated in *danza de la sota*," a *danza* instructor once told me as I prepared to interview him in his home in Solaga. I turned around and saw a mustard-colored market bag. Through my grandmother's advice and my encounters with community members, I have come to realize that in and for my *pueblo*, I am more than myself. The relationships I form with other Solagueños are grounded in longer genealogies I inherited from the bonds my parents and ancestors have with other Solagueños, as well as through the bonds I have cultivated through my own *convivencia*.[27] While this type of recognition may be or become commonplace for Solagueños and members of the diaspora who learn to see each other in similar ways, it can be a culture shock to diasporic children and youth who grow up in an individualistic society like the United States. This different understanding of the self subsequently shapes the experience of diasporic returnees who may ordinarily see themselves as individuals rather than as a part of a collective.

Language and Return Visits

Colonization, globalization, and migration have created a world that continues to shape Solagueño lives in the hometown and diaspora. While Solaga is a Zapotec-speaking town, many Solagueño parents prioritize their children's Spanish language acquisition thinking that their children will be better off being more fluent in this European language rather than their mother tongue. Felix has unique insight into language use in the community. He is a native Zapotec speaker from Solaga and an Indigenous language instructor at a local school. Felix's Zapotec-speaking ability and his teaching position are a result of shifting language ideologies in the community. While as children his parents' generation was discouraged through corporal punishment from speaking Zapotec,[28] by the time Felix attended the same elementary school, the school required students to take a Zapotec writing course. In his capacity as Indigenous language instructor, moreover, Felix now facilitates academic and community spaces where Indigenous youth can learn and speak their Indigenous languages. However, language ideologies that privilege European languages over Indigenous languages persist among Solagueños in the hometown and in the diaspora.

While Solagueño schools have become sites where Zapotec use is encouraged, some Solagueños raise their children as monolingual Spanish speakers, believing this will be most beneficial to their children. "They think speaking an Indigenous language is useless. That it is not important. That's why they would rather only teach them Spanish," Felix explained. Children's personalities also determine how likely they are to speak their mother tongue. Within Felix's family, Zapotec-speaking ability varied. Felix, his parents, and one of his siblings speak Zapotec, while his youngest sibling does not. When I asked him why he thought this was the case, Felix rationalized:

> We [the Zapotec-speaking siblings] enjoyed speaking the language. That's why I think we speak Zapotec. In the other case, I don't know if it doesn't grab her attention or I don't know what it is.

Despite being born in Solaga and being raised in a Zapotec-speaking household, ideal conditions for Zapotec language retention, Felix's sister has shown little interest in speaking the language. Living in a bilingual town allows individuals to be monolingual. While Solagueños who remain in their hometown could viably choose to remain monolingual in their Indigenous language, his sister's preference for Spanish—a language of power in Mexico—may demonstrate an understanding of the Spanish language as one that not only allows her to communicate within her hometown, but one that may also provide her with opportunities outside of the hometown.

Migration to Oaxaca City, Mexico City, and Los Angeles has exacerbated language loss among members of the Solagueño diaspora. On the other hand, emigration from Solaga has led the town to become a trilingual community with Solagueños speaking a combination of Zapotec, Spanish, and English. Like the Mixtec diaspora,[29] diasporic Solagueño families have shifted toward Spanish use. This shift may be a result of the prejudice Indigenous Latinx immigrants and their children may experience at the hands of non-Indigenous Latinx immigrants, as well as a concern that speaking an Indigenous language might impede diasporic Indigenous children's integration into American culture.[30] Felix shared that some of his U.S.-born cousins understood Zapotec, but did not speak the language. To avoid any confusion, Felix communicates with his cousins in Spanish, a language they can understand and speak, during their visits. While living in a multilingual setting is not new for Solagueños, tensions between locals and diasporic youth may arise over English language use during return trips. During our conversation, Felix made an observation about visiting diasporic children and youth:

> What I've seen is that they come here and only speak English. Only English. It seems ... disrespectful. I don't know. We're in a *pueblo* ... the least they could do is speak Spanish. Like when we run into a group, we don't know what they're saying.

I made a face at Felix and was ready to defend my peers by pointing out how some Solagueño locals have conversations in Zapotec about visiting youths or their family in front of them with the assumption that the youths will not understand them. Felix, however, laughed and quickly added,

"I think the same thing happens when we speak *zapoteco* ... maybe." At Felix's mention of Solagueño locals not understanding returnees, the reverse situation quickly sprang to my mind and showed in my facial expression. As a member of the Los Angeles diaspora, I tend to speak English when speaking with other returnees. This, however, is a matter of habit, rather than a slight toward Solagueño locals. Indeed, English is the language in which most diasporic children and youth are most proficient and consequently the most comfortable to speak.

I have encountered diasporic youth who held similar views to Felix's views around language, albeit in their case Zapotec. While my ability to speak Spanish and Zapotec keeps me in the loop with locals during my visits to Solaga, and my ability to speak English also allows me to converse with other Angelenos visiting Solaga, the same is not the case for all locals and visitors. Felix pointed out the tensions that arise between locals and returnees when someone does not speak at least one of the three languages spoken by members of the Solagueño diaspora.

While Felix's observations were focused on language use among members of the diaspora, his statement reflects cultural differences he observed between locals and returnees. Throughout the interview, Felix referred to visiting diasporic youths and adults as either *"ustedes"* (you all) or *"ellos"* (they/them). In the statement above, he used *"ellos,"* excluding me from the returnees who only conversed in English. Since our conversation was entirely in Spanish, I adhered to Felix's expectations of how returnees should behave in Solaga. In speaking Spanish—one of the two languages most local Solagueños speak and understand—and socializing with locals, I was "being respectful" of the *pueblo* and its inhabitants.[31] Conflict over language use is not exclusive to Solaga. In the context of Mexico City, Mexican locals may harass deportees or returnees for speaking English in public places, where they expect them to converse in Spanish.[32] Vera-Rosas and Guerrero partially attribute this reaction to the legacy of U.S. intervention and empire in Mexico. While this may also explain Felix's apprehension about returnees' use of English, his acceptance of Spanish as a lingua franca demonstrates that his reaction may extend beyond a decolonial critique and instead be rooted in what he may have seen as some youths' refusal to *convivir*, or socialize with locals.

In the Sierra Juarez, notions of respect are tied to *convivencia*.[33] Gross's work on religious conflict between Catholics and Protestants demonstrates that community members strive to respect differing religious values for the sake of social cohesion. The ability to *convivir* in spite of religious differences allows for a sense of social cohesion that is necessary for the viability of community membership under *usos y costumbres*, wherein Indigenous Oaxacan communities decide the norms and practice through which their communities are governed. Like *usos y costumbres*, expectations for *convivencia* are also place-based, that is, the community decides who belongs, how they are able claim membership in the community, and how they should behave while in the community. Thus, socializing with Los Angeles–based Solagueños and speaking English, something that is commonplace for diasporic children and youth, may be perceived as a slight to Solagueños who may interpret this as a lack of respect toward locals. In Felix's estimation, when diasporic youth limit their social interactions in Solaga to their English-speaking peers and speak a language locals are likely unfamiliar with, they foreclose opportunities to *convivir*, build relationships with other Solagueños, and be integrated into the community. From a local perspective, exclusively socializing with other returnees may defeat the purpose of visiting Solaga, when youth return or are encouraged to travel to experience the place and its people.[34]

Although Felix understood the reasoning behind local parents' apprehension about conversing with their children in Zapotec, he did not seem to extend this reasoning to similar situations Solagueños encounter in diaspora. As with other immigrant communities in the United States, the normal pattern of language loss within three immigrant generations is also part of the Solagueño immigrant experience.[35] This is further exacerbated among Indigenous immigrants who may be reluctant to teach their children their native languages due to the belief that speaking an Indigenous language could potentially hinder the incorporation of their children into American society[36] and as a result of the language ideologies instilled in them as children. Diasporic children and youth's experiences of bullying and discrimination may further dissuade them from speaking their native languages.[37]

As in other immigrant communities,[38] proficiency in their community's languages shapes diasporic youth's return visits. Some returnees may understand and even speak Zapotec, while others cannot. As Felix notes, conversations in English among visiting youth cause suspicion among the locals, who more than likely do not understand what returning youth are saying. The same applies with visiting youth who do not speak Zapotec and are suspicious of locals' conversations in Zapotec. A few days before that year's *Virgen del Carmen fiesta*, I was running some errands in Solaga when I stumbled upon a group of English-speaking teenagers in *El Centro*, Solaga's town square. As I walked behind them, I heard them discussing their encounter with a couple of locals who had apparently had a side conversation in Zapotec while talking to the visiting youths in Spanish. There was a sense of outrage among the teenagers since they were convinced that the locals were gossiping about them to their faces. Felix's observations following the *fiesta* reminded me of this incident. While I had neither seen nor heard the interaction they were discussing, I have seen and been part of similar interactions, especially with locals who are unaware of my own ability to speak Zapotec.

I learned to speak Zapotec when my maternal grandmother, cousin, and uncle emigrated to Los Angeles around a year after my first trip to Solaga. Overnight, my home became a bilingual Spanish and Zapotec household. Prior to this, my parents only spoke Spanish in our home. As I grew older, I noticed my father would deny being Oaxacan when people inquired about his background. This attempt to disassociate from his Indigenous identity likely affected his decision to only speak Spanish at home. I began to understand Zapotec at some point during the six months we lived together. I realized people usually spoke the language when they did not want me to understand their conversations. I let my family know that I knew what they were saying to ensure they would not talk about me. To encourage me to listen in on their conversations my uncle ended all his sentences saying, "kon llechhobo ka," or "we'll just tell her that." His strategy worked and I soon began to master the language. The return trips I eventually embarked on once my grandmother returned to Solaga increased my fluency. Since then, my ability to speak Zapotec sparks amusement in my family and curiosity among Solagueños. Solagueños that have heard about my Zapotec-speaking ability sometimes speak to me in Zapotec in hopes that I will respond in Zapotec. When they hear me speak Zapotec, some marvel at the fact that I sound like a native speaker or that I speak the language when many local youths cannot or choose not to speak the language.

Although I am usually amused by remarks people make in front of me oblivious to the fact that I am fluent in Zapotec, some visiting youth find similar situations uncomfortable. Arturo, a 19-year-old second-generation Solagueño, shared that he felt unwelcome when Solagueños assumed he did not speak Zapotec because he was born in the United States: "They assume you don't understand *zapoteco* and they're talking about a lot of stuff. Sometimes they talk about you and sometimes they're like, 'Oh, isn't that this and this's son.' Like that's just ... I don't feel unwelcome but I don't always feel totally welcome." Arturo's insight shows what encounters between returnees and locals usually entail. While it is commonplace for locals to locate youths by naming their parents, a youth who is unaccustomed to these conventions may become uncomfortable, especially if locals end up "talking about" or gossiping about a returnee or their family. These interactions shed light on why some returnees may choose to socialize with each other: they may be avoiding uncomfortable situations in which they do not (or are assumed not to) speak the same language or encounter a type of relationality they are unaccustomed to in the United States.

For Solagueño immigrants' children who grow up in the U.S., visits to Solaga may heighten the differences between locals and Solagueños born or raised in Los Angeles. Linguistically, the children of Indigenous immigrants not only contend with the legacy of colonization on their parents' ancestral land but must also contend with being socialized in the immigrant receiving society and how these forces compound to shape their experiences in the hometown.

Gendered Returns

Scholars have noted how transnational migration can challenge gender norms immigrants bring with them from their countries of origin. Upon migrating to the United States, Lynn Stephen notes, Oaxacan immigrants "readjust their expectations and understandings of the gendered relations of work and home. Economic survival in the United States for those working minimum wage jobs requires both husbands and wives work one and often two jobs."[39] Many female immigrants find themselves on a more equal footing than their male counterparts in their new capacity as breadwinners.[40] This, in turn, provides their children with a set of gendered expectation that may differ from those in their parents' society of origin. In addition to changes in gendered relations, the political and social environment for immigrants and their children in their new homes transforms gendered cultural practices Indigenous immigrants bring with them to the United States.[41] Oaxacan girls' and women's participation in *danzas* and brass bands show a shift in cultural practices from those that were previously male-centered to ones that women transformed to be more inclusive in diaspora.[42] Shifting ideas about gender are of course not limited to the diaspora. In transborder communities, "ideas, behaviors, and social capital (skills, knowledge) flow both out of the home community and into it, encouraging people ... to try on new ideas about politics, culture, and even gendered roles."[43] In the Zapotec community of Yalalag, for example, the United States has come to symbolize a place where young people can have more autonomy and be free from the criticism and judgment leveled by their community.[44] In returning to their parents' *pueblo*, the daughters of immigrants are often confronted with a degree of social control that they find more stifling.[45] Young women visiting Solaga must contend with gender norms in the sending community, which, as Yalalteco youth do, they may regard as more restrictive than in Los Angeles. Despite these differences, many of the young women I spoke to or encountered during my time in Solaga learn to navigate different gendered expectations and visit their *pueblo* on an almost annual basis.

A couple of days after the conclusion of the *Virgen del Carmen* festivities, I met up with Rebecca and her cousin Ana, who was also from Los Angeles, in *El Centro*. Rebecca asked Ana and me to accompany her to her house where we would be more comfortable than standing in the town's outdoor market structure. After a short walk, we reached the house in which Rebecca's grandparents lived. I had seen Rebecca at community events and family parties in Los Angeles my entire life. I assumed that, like myself, she had been born in the United States. It was not until we officially met during this trip that I found out that she had been born in Solaga and brought to the United States as a child. She and her parents had since been able to adjust their status. Rebecca, then 23 years old, had been traveling to Solaga for the

Virgen del Carmen festivities since she was 7 years old. As we ate tamales and sipped on the coffee her grandmother insisted we have while we chatted, Rebecca discussed her return trips to the community as part of the Solagueño youth band, *Solaga USA Oaxaca*:

> I came with the band in '04 and '08. It's something I'm never going to forget. Everyone was so excited. We were so pumped up ... playing for our grandparents ... coming from so far to an annual feast when a lot of people come.

Rebecca's recollections demonstrate the special significance Solagueños across generations attach to return trips that involve participating in transborder practices of belonging that connect youth to their culture and family, including partaking in a *danza* or playing in the brass band.

As Rebecca noted, engaging in these activities in the presence of visitors and family members makes these occasions particularly meaningful. In Solaga, *danzas* rely on children and youth's participation. Children and youth spend weeks practicing in preparation for patron saint celebrations and perform for several hours a day during the five-day celebration. Participating in the Solagueño brass band entails a similar commitment, with band members practicing for community or neighboring community events and performing for the entirety of those celebrations, which often includes very little rest and spending almost a week away from their hometown. While members of *Solaga USA* likely returned to the comfort of their parents' or grandparents' homes in Solaga, the distance they traveled, the *promesa* or sacred vow they made to the patron saint, and the joy they put forth in participating in these practices demonstrate diasporic children and youth's commitment to the patron saint and the community in a way that is legible to their *pueblo*.

Visiting Solaga throughout her childhood, adolescence, and into adulthood has given Rebecca a unique perspective on how return visits can change over the course of one's life. She fondly remembered enjoying traveling to Solaga as a child: "You were free to be wherever you wanted to be. You're not at risk of danger here." In Solaga, Los Angeles–based children are able to *convivir* with relatives and friends across town with minimal adult supervision. This is in stark contrast to diasporic children and youth's experiences growing up in Los Angeles, where their parents attempted to protect their children from the issues afflicting their inner-city neighborhoods by insisting they avoid going outside or involving them in extracurricular activities that would keep them busy and safe, as I detailed in Chapter 2. In a small town like Solaga, individuals, including children, can be quickly located as the customary greeting includes inquiring where people are headed. Compared to their neighborhood in Los Angeles, such supervision may provide diasporic children and youth with a style of care that ensures they can have more freedom to socialize with peers and relatives throughout the community.

Attitudes toward small town life may shift as diasporic children, particularly female children, mature. Rebecca shared some of the differences between her trips to Solaga as a child and her more recent ones:

> There's curfew. You have to be home by 8 [p.m.]. When I was younger, I didn't mind because where was I going to be, you know? But now, you know, I want to hang out with the friends around town. Another one of the disadvantages is it's a small town. Small town big talk, everybody finds out about everything.

Rebecca has continued returning to Solaga now that she is not a part of the Los Angeles–based youth band. Through her return trips, she has created and maintained solid relationships with local musicians and community members, as well as other diasporic Solagueños she has met during *fiestas*. For Rebecca, the differences noted between the small town of Solaga and the urban metropolis of Los Angeles become more salient as children, particularly female children, mature. In Solaga, public space is limited to the town square, which includes the town's municipal palace, a Catholic church, outdoor market structures, and a basketball court. Coupled with an early curfew, visiting youth seemingly have less time, places, and opportunities to socialize with their friends and relatives than in Los Angeles. This was not an issue for Rebecca as a child; however, as she has matured, the repercussions for engaging in activities that were acceptable as a child and are now deemed inappropriate have begun to shape her experiences of Solaga. In the Sierra Juarez region, behavior deemed inappropriate for women includes being unchaperoned, socializing with men, and dating.[46]

Diasporic Solagueñas must learn to maneuver between the social realities and expectations they contend with in Los Angeles and Solaga.

Becoming the subject of town gossip may damage a young woman and her family's reputation in the *pueblo*. Whether "good" or "bad," a person's actions are reflections of their entire family. This construction of self and the family differs from the one diasporic children and youth are accustomed to in the United States, where "youths are encouraged to be economically and socially independent to make decisions for themselves, and to believe that each individual is the best judge of what he or she wants and should do."[47] In traveling to Solaga, U.S.-reared youth must adapt to a collective society where they are expected to acquiesce to the needs and values of the group for the sake of social cohesion.[48] These different expectations may lead some second-generation Solagueñas to modify their behavior for the purpose of their visit. One returnee, Alicia, a 22-year-old member of the second generation, confessed to not drinking socially with her peers for fear that rumors would spread about her and that her family would become the subject of town gossip.

In some instances, Solagueña relatives may attempt to intervene to salvage diasporic women's reputation. Valentina recalled an instance when her cousin Gabriela, who was visiting from Los Angeles, stopped by her house in Solaga:

> Gabriela came by and my aunt was there. I was so embarrassed … my aunt started to lecture her about her drinking. She was like, "They might say, 'It's just a beer' but it's not. I know it's different where you come from, but you have to remember where you are. Try not to drink when you're here."

Importantly, this encounter shows townspeople's competing views about women's drinking. While some may encourage women to drink, others see this encouragement as a test. For local Solagueñas and by extension visiting women, their own and their family's reputation is at stake. Valentina's aunt also acknowledges that diasporic Solagueñas may abide by different standards in the place they now live. Nevertheless, because they are in Solaga, women like Gabriela are encouraged to modify their behavior. Gabriela is among the visiting Solagueñas who refuse to modify their behavior to meet community norms.

Indigenous scholars hold varying stances on gossip's role in Indigenous communities. Martínez Luna identifies *chisme* (or gossip) as a form of *convivencia* and connects *chisme* to orality, which he considers an essential part of Zapotec communal existence.[49] Deborah Miranda draws on the writing of Leslie Marmon Silko and argues that gossip is "at the heart of good storytelling as well as a strong Indigenous community."[50] Miranda and Silko both posit that the subject of gossip itself is less important than its function: the telling and retelling of a story holds a community together and creates bonds of intimacy beyond kinship and connects Indigenous worlds despite constantly shifting circumstances. Silko asserts that these stories ground individuals to things, people, and identities they can refer to when something similar happens to them. In doing so, they will never feel alone or lost.[51] In the Chatino communities of Cieneguilla and San Juan, community members have a complicated relationship with gossip—they simultaneously profess hating it, while feeling disrespected if they are denied this information.[52] While Solagueño *chisme* may certainly include harmful gossip, as a form of *convivencia, chisme* creates and reinforces community and interpersonal bonds and allows for the sharing of community news. For diasporic youth growing up in a Western context, where gossip is regarded as malicious,[53] this form of *convivencia*—where community members inquire into where you are headed, your and your family's well-being, as well as openly discuss recent events in one's life—may initially seem intrusive. For example, the summer after my father passed, when community members stopped to greet me, they would inquire about my mother and sisters and remark how only a few months had passed since my father's death. They would comment on how unfortunate it must be for me that my father died. These frequent occurrences and being unaccustomed to this in an American setting stirred up my grief and made me uncomfortable. In retrospect, however, these encounters show not only how Solagueños viewed me as a person—as an extension of my parents—but also their awareness of recent losses in my family and how as a daughter I must still have been mourning my father's loss. Rather than injurious gossip or *chisme*, their remarks were an acknowledgment of my state of mind and my loss and indeed a recognition of my humanity. For diasporic children and youth who are unfamiliar with this way of relating, these situations may be exacerbated by linguistic and cultural differences between locals and diasporic Solagueños.

Children and youth's experiences in their homeland may determine the likelihood they will continue engaging in return trips. As Rebecca's observations demonstrate, these experiences may change as children mature. Patron saint celebrations allow youth to engage in the practices they have engaged with in diaspora and provide opportunities for them to interact with members of the diaspora living outside of Los Angeles, as well as with community members living in Solaga. This experience offers opportunity for positive experiences in the homeland, but may also lead to tension among visiting youth and townspeople. Still, diasporic returnees from Oaxaca City, Mexico City, and Los Angeles bring with them the values through which they are socialized. Townspeople may thus be more accepting of the differing social realities of visiting Solagueños or may actively encourage them to abide by community standards. Despite these tensions, children and youth's relationship to Solaga and the relationships they build with family and friends may keep many of them going back into adulthood.

Rebecca's return trips have given her a perspective of what *convivencia* in Solaga may be like at different points in her life. The freedom she enjoyed as a girl was replaced by restrictions based on her gender. These were reinforced by the threat of becoming the subject of the town's gossip. Still, Rebecca and other young women continue visiting despite these new restrictions. Toward the end of our conversation, Ana chimed in that she continued to return because "gossip doesn't play a big factor for me. Visiting the relatives [in Solaga] is more important." Opportunities to *convivir* with her friends and members in Solaga motivate women like Ana to continue visiting the community, despite the gossip their behavior might cause. However, for diasporic Solagueñas who start to engage in return trips as adults, gender norms in the community may come as more of a shock. Women may acquiesce to these norms, reject them, or decide to not return to Solaga.

Conclusion

Through return trips, diasporic children and youth can live among and engage with community members in the hometown, which allows them to *convivir* or build and maintain relations with people and place. Youth experiences in diaspora inevitably shape their return trips to Solaga. As they mature, youth learn that their ability to *convivir* may change across their lifetime. This is especially so for women who engaged in return trips from an early age. Linguistic differences further exacerbate tensions between locals and returnees, with both parties suspicious of linguistic choices among community members. While these differences certainly shape return visits, the ultimate issue at hand is Solagueños' ability to *convivir* with community members. *Convivencia* is critical to Indigenous sociality and relationality and entails an experiential knowledge of people and place. Opportunities for *convivencia* for displaced Indigenous peoples, particularly those that have had to migrate without authorization, remain limited. Nevertheless, Indigenous immigrants have found ways to circumvent barriers to their movement. Undocumented immigrants continue to transgress state attempts to control their movement by mobilizing their community members' legal statuses and the mobility this bestows on them. In mobilizing these statuses, Solagueños refuse settler borders and challenge state-imposed restrictions to Indigenous peoples' movement. While tensions may arise during return trips, Solagueños' practices of *convivencia* challenge settler attempts to eliminate their way of life by disrupting their ability to remain in and eventually return to their homeland.

FOUR

Music Follows Serranos

MY MOTHER, SISTERS, AND I arrived at a banquet hall in South Central Los Angeles. In 2014, the feast day in honor of Saint Andrew, the Catholic saint after whom San Andrés Solaga is named, fell on a Sunday. In Solaga, patron saint festivities are observed on set dates. In diaspora, however, celebrations are held on weekends. On this occasion, the Solagueño community in Los Angeles was able to celebrate our town's patron saint on his feast day at the same time as our *paisanos* in our hometown. When we arrived at the venue, we tried to figure out where to take the water and soda cases I brought for the *fiesta*; we ran into a band member's father who helped us carry the drinks from my car into the venue. The woman at the door, my mother's second cousin and childhood friend, started writing my mother's name down as the donor but my mother insisted she write my name down, since I was the actual donor. The list was already one page long and included the names of other Solagueños, along with the items they donated.[1] By the time we walked into the venue, Mass had started and most of the available seats were taken.

Patron saints are honored with *misas oaxaqueñas* (Oaxacan Masses), for which a Oaxacan brass band and a choir are needed. During this celebration, the Los Angeles–based Solagueño youth band, *Banda Juvenil Solaga USA Oaxaca*, performed during the Mass, while a choir, made up of six first-generation immigrant women, a first-generation man, and a young woman that appeared to be a member of the second generation, sang. As I would eventually realize during my fieldwork, like many community functions this was a multigenerational endeavor. People continued to arrive throughout the duration of Mass. At one point, individuals started grabbing folding chairs as they came into the venue and placing them where they wished to sit. During the homily, the deacon praised *Solaga USA* for participating in the religious celebration and said he hoped the children of Solagueños born in the United States would continue preserving their parents' traditions.

Once the Mass ended, the band played "Las Mañanitas" and "Celebremos Con Gusto Señores" in honor of San Andrés's feast day before band members ventured outside. Then Carlos, a 46-year-old Solagueño immigrant who emcees many Solagueño events, welcomed those in attendance, who included Solagueño immigrants, their children, and their grandchildren, as well as individuals from other Oaxacan towns. He related to attendees how Solagueños came to Los Angeles with the goal of going back to their hometown, but this changed once they began having children in the United States. Carlos's comments were especially poignant because after over two decades of living in Los Angeles and becoming a successful small business owner, he has not been able to adjust his status and return to his hometown.[2] He concluded his speech by announcing that *Banda San Jeronimo Zoochina L.A.* would arrive soon and encouraged attendees to enjoy some refreshments in the meantime.

We made our way outside and found the venue's parking lot covered with party tents. Inside these tents were tables with bread, *tamales,* coffee, and *champurrado,*[3] as well as tables and chairs for people to sit after they received their food and drink. Once attendees finished eating, they headed back inside. By the time we went back inside, *Banda San Jeronimo Zoochina L.A.* had arrived and played "Las Mañanitas" at the altar that had been set up with the image of *San Andrés.* The band then played a *diana* in honor of San Andrés and sat in their designated area, where they continued to play until the *danza* was ready to perform. Carlos took the stage to present the *danza* and to express his delight that so many *Serranos,* people from the Sierra Norte region of Oaxaca where Solaga and Zoochina are located, lived in Los Angeles because "*la musica sigue a los Serranos,*" or "music follows Serranos."

For Solagueños, music allows community members across generations to maintain a connection to their ancestral homeland and to foster relationships among themselves and other Serranos in Los Angeles.[4] *Bi wekuell* are community members who are highly regarded for their musical talent and the web of relations they are able to foster through their musical practices.[5] In Solaga, the service musicians provide for the community is so valued that they do not have to serve in other positions of the town's *cargo* system so long as they are active in the municipal band.[6] As *bi wekuell,* Solagueño musicians across space, time, and generation participate in the co-construction of knowledges developed in Indigenous communities over millennia.[7] *Bi wekuell's* musical expertise and sonic practices permeate all aspects of Solagueño communal life and allow Solagueños and the larger Serrano community in Los Angeles to engage with their homeland's soundscapes.[8] These soundscapes—along with linguistic, cultural, and culinary practices— facilitate Indigenous place-making practices that connect immigrants in Los Angeles with their *pueblos.*[9] Through soundscapes that include music, language, and sounds associated with their hometowns, Indigenous people can engage in and show belonging through millennial and ever-evolving forms of Indigenous communal life.

This chapter highlights the role of *bi wekuell* in creating the sonic space through which Serranos can practice *comunalidad,* or collective community life.[10] I argue that the auditory culture that follows Serranos—and which they continue to develop in diaspora—allows them to create sonic spaces in which they can affirm and build a communal sense of belonging. While not all Serranos are *bene wekuell,* we form part of a shared sonic space by knowing and coming together to engage with brass bands' repertoires. A focus on aurality[11] allows us to explore how diasporic Indigenous children and youth use music and sounds as communicative practices to engage in Solagueño and Serrano communal practices. By centering autochthonous modalities of communication (including voice, music, and dance) through which Indigenous peoples construct their social world, Indigenous youth challenge Western traditions that have historically privileged the written word to dismiss Indigenous communicative practices.[12] For Zapotec peoples, Zapotec thought, dance, and spiritual practices are embedded within musical expressions.[13] So too is the landscape of their homeland. For

Indigenous peoples living in diaspora, moreover, the aural—or what we hear—has the capacity to transform the reality of what we see.[14] Thus, while we may not be able to be physically present in our communities, Serranos in "separate spaces can savor the same sounds."[15]

This chapter details the aural modalities through which displaced Solagueño children and youth index belonging to their *pueblo*, including music and sound. Settler attempts to eradicate Indigenous cultures and languages across the Americas have led to language loss in many Indigenous communities, and the children of Indigenous immigrants, including members of *Solaga USA*, are a testament to this legacy. While many *bi wekuell* may not be able to communicate in their parents' native language, they engage in autochthonous modalities of communication that emerged as forms of resistance to the colonial surveillance and subjugation of native peoples and languages.[16] Here, I examine how music allows Indigenous children and youth to form and sustain ties to their communities of origin and to create spaces in which Indigenous immigrants can transmit their cultural and community values to their children away from their homeland. The deterritorialization and reterritorialization of Oaxacan aural practices allow Indigenous immigrants and their children to replenish their Indigenous identities away from their ethnic homeland despite living in anti-immigrant and anti-Indigenous settler colonial contexts. In processes of identity formation for diasporic Solagueño youth in Los Angeles, communal practices allow Indigenous children and youth to connect their places of settlement with their places of origin. These practices are necessary as Indigenous immigrants and their children contend with displacement and migration from their places of origin, as well as state and police violence, economic exploitation, and racial discrimination.[17]

Sensing Solaga

One night before band practice, my cousin Matias and I grabbed dinner at a Mexican restaurant near *Solaga USA*'s rehearsal space. Likely inspired by his meal, Matias invited me to think of the relationship between food, place, and memory. When you eat something, he told me, it reminds you of the time you first tried it. People eat beignets, Matias continued, because it reminds them of their adventures in New Orleans or France. Music, he suggested, had a similar capacity to evoke memories:

> It's the music of Oaxaca ... it reminds you of the melodies you heard at the parties in Oaxaca. You know ... dancing in the basketball courts because that's where you dance ... I don't think that someone that hasn't visited there, that hasn't really heard the music there, that hasn't really smelled the bread, the coffee there—everything smells different there. And when you come back, everything smells different because it reminds you of the place that you want to be in because you're smelling it here. They're memories that you hold of being there. The reason you listen to the music is because you remember being there. You remember listening to there. You want to listen to it, make it feel like how you were over there. You want to close your eyes, listen to the band ... picture yourself dancing with your cousin, with your aunt, with your friend, or with your girlfriend. You know? To me, that's why music exists. To remind you of a certain point in time.

Through his observation, Matias encouraged me to think of the sensorial experience of being in Solaga, the town from which our parents migrated.[18] While Matias and I were born in Los Angeles, we have both traveled to and formed memories in our parents' hometown. These sensorial memories, Matias suggested, inform how Solagueños across generations experience the smells, sounds, and tastes of Solaga in our ancestral homeland and in diaspora. The sensorial experiences Matias associates with the *fiesta* in Solaga are experienced differently by local and diasporic Solagueños and non-Serrano visitors.[19] Return trips allow diasporic Solagueños to *convivir* or live in and engage with Solaga and Solagueños. Key to diasporic experiences of the homeland are with whom these experiences are shared—*paisanos* and kin.

Return visits allow parental figures in the hometown to connect diasporic Indigenous children and youth with different and ancestral ways of knowing and being in the world, including the preparation and consumption of ancestral foods.[20] Diasporic Solagueños regularly consume Solagueño food staples and listen to and dance to *jarabes* in Los Angeles. Matias, however, stresses the special significance of experiencing these activities in our communal territory. Indeed, opportunities to *convivir* in the *pueblo* and with our families are the reasons many of our parents encourage us to visit our ancestral homeland. Through return trips, diasporic children and youth engage in communal enjoyment *in* the communal territory. In doing so, they engage in the sensations particular to the *fiesta* as our parents and ancestors once did. Through our embodied engagement with ancestral memory, we are able to learn and transmit ancestral knowledge, including the joy and satisfaction of participating in communal life.

Music allows us to remember what it *feels* like to be in Solaga. If we close our eyes and listen, we transport ourselves to the place longed for by Solagueños across generations. For some community members, including Matias's undocumented parents, the memories that *wekuell* are able to elicit are as close as they can get to experiencing their hometown in the flesh. Since undocumented Solagueños are not able to travel to Solaga with the guarantee they will be able to return due to their unauthorized status, patron saint festivities in Los Angeles are their only opportunity to partake in patron saint festivities away from their hometown. Through their musicianship and through their transborder movement, diasporic wekuell are crucial to creating the sonic space through which Solagueños can experience and support their hometown.

Earlier in our conversation, Matias had reflected on the importance of diasporic youth to the Oaxacan community. He observed:

> If Oaxacan kids stop going to the party, the traditions would get lost. The money the [hometown] organizations get [from the fundraisers], they'll start losing the support ... the contact here. Let's say from one day to another all the Oaxacan kids stop going to the parties. Where has the tradition gone? It'll be forgotten.

As Matias spoke, I, too, started imagining community events without the children of Oaxacan immigrants. I responded, "There's no band!" Still picturing a world without Oaxacan youth, Matias responded:

> Yeah. It'll be unknown! Like "Where are you from again?" "Oaxaca." "I've never heard of that place." But because there are a lot of kids here, a lot of teachers are like, "Oh, you're Oaxacan? You must play music." So, it makes the pueblos known. It's representing Oaxaca and without it, it's just another lost place.

Matias demonstrates how intertwined Solagueño diasporic life is with the activities of the Solagueño youth band. Matias credits youth and the band with keeping the community together by maintaining contact among Solagueños and by sustaining Solaga's Los Angeles–based hometown associations, which provide support for Solagueño immigrants and for community projects in the hometown. While most Solagueños live in the Koreatown and Mid-City neighborhoods of Los Angeles, community events hosted by *Solaga USA* set a time and a date in which Solagueños can come together to honor or support their community. For displaced peoples accustomed to communal life, these events create spaces in which the community can momentarily experience their hometown as they and their ancestors once did. Matias again highlights the role of the aural in representing Oaxaca and its *pueblos*. The music, he argued, is what distinguishes Oaxacans from other groups.[21]

Through their participation in the Solagueño youth band, Oaxacan youth not only learn that music allows for an embodied experience of place but *wekuell* become essential to the enactment of Solagueño forms of social organization in diaspora. To be in good standing and claim membership in a Zapotec community, community members must be physically present and active in community life through participation in the *cargo* system, *gozona* and *tequio*, or mutual aid and communal labor.[22] Together, these practices promote *comunalidad*, or collective cooperation within a *pueblo* and between *pueblos*. Migration, however, has brought about changes to how Indigenous peoples stake claims to belonging to their hometown. In some diasporic Indigenous communities, obligations to the *cargo* system have been transferred to hometown associations, which in turn become the institutions through which immigrants maintain community ties.[23] Some diasporic children of immigrants demonstrate their attachment to their community of origin through their participation in hometown associations.[24] Unlike Zoochinenses in Nicolas's study, however, U.S.-born Solagueños' community membership does not rely on their participation in their community's hometown associations. Still, as Matias points out, diasporic youth are integral to the viability of Los Angeles–based hometown associations and community-specific endeavors through their ability to bring the community together through music.

From the Solaga Sound to the Sounds of Solaga

The Los Angeles–based Solagueño youth band has undergone many changes since its inception, including changes in directors. Antonio, the Solagueño immigrant man who had proposed the community form a youth band composed of the children of Solagueño, served as the band's first director. Guillermo was among the youth that were recruited during this time. Guillermo recalled how through Antonio's musical instruction, he and his fellow *bi wekuell* were able to develop what he calls the *Solaga style*:

> We made a name for ourselves, too. Here, among the other Oaxacan bands. The Solaga band ... because we were a lot ... we had a good sound. They said that we sounded like we had the style because the teacher who taught us, he came from Solaga so he had the style too. So he taught us the same style. So when we started playing, we developed that style that sounds like Solaga style. You know? That sound. We got that sound down.

Earlier, Matias discussed how music distinguishes Oaxacan youth from the rest of the student population in Los Angeles schools. Here, Guillermo indicates how the Solagueño youth band developed a reputation among other Los Angeles–based Oaxacan bands through the distinct style they were able to develop under Antonio's tutelage that harkened back to their hometown's municipal band.

In mentioning the municipal band's style, like Matias, Guillermo evokes memories of sounds, more specifically a style of playing, from the homeland. Isaac, a Solagueño from Oaxaca City who occasionally plays with Solaga's municipal band, explained Solaga's distinct style.

> What makes Solaga's band unique, from my perspective, is the different *maestros* they've had. You know, they've had teachers from Toton[tepec] ... Yalalag and as they were forming musicians they gave a tone especially to *sones* and as the years went by there has been renowned musicians that have also contributed to this. Now each time Solaga's band plays *jarabes*, the rhythm ... the flavor that they put into it is recognizable, especially the trumpet players. When they play "La Hermanita" or "El Son del Toro" they give it a beautiful style.

While Solaga's *maestros* were instrumental in the development of the Solaga sound, musicians are also key to the execution and transmission of the sound in diaspora.

For Guillermo, these sounds extend beyond the aural; they are also familial. On his father's side, Guillermo and his sibling are part of a long lineage of Solagueño *wekuell*. His grandfather was part of the municipal band and his cousins are current band members. Through hearing about and witnessing their experiences, Guillermo has been able to gauge the status of Solaga's municipal band in the Sierra Juarez. Having traveled with them for another town's summer festivities, he witnessed how the municipal band was treated like "royalty." The ability to reproduce the "Solaga style" afforded the Solagueño youth band a similar status among Oaxacan bands and the Oaxacan community in Los Angeles.

While learning from a Solaga-trained musician may have influenced youths to develop a distinctive style at the outset of the band's formation, diasporic *wekuell* have incorporated their own sonic experiences into the soundscapes they create at Solagueño community events. Their contributions are influenced by their musical training in other genres,[25] as well as their return trips to Solaga. After Jesse, *Solaga USA's* bass drum player, returned from a patron saint celebration in Solaga, he started adding the sound of *cohetes* (firecrackers) to *jarabes* during the youth band's performances. In Solaga, *cohetes* are set off to indicate different moments in the festivities, including the arrival and departure of a visiting band and the end of a prayer service or Mass. Community members that are familiar with the schedule of the day's events can mark time and where we are in the festivities through the sounds of the *cohetes* no matter what part of town they are in or what they are doing. More generally, firecrackers also indicate that we are celebrating. On the eve of the main feast day, *cohetes* and fireworks are set off to honor the patron saint while the local and visiting bands play *jarabes*. Jesse imitated *cohetes* by using his mouth to whistle and hitting the *bombo*, or bass drum. The whistle mimicked the sound of a firecracker when it has been lit and soars into the air, while hitting the *bombo* created the sound of the firecracker exploding. Jesse produced a sound combination, a *cohete* being set off during a *jarabe*, that is almost exclusive to patron saint celebrations in the Sierra Juarez. By mimicking a *cohete* during a *jarabe* in

Los Angeles, Jesse uses sound to elucidate memories or feelings of being in Solaga during the height of the community's festivities.

During my time with *Solaga USA*, I became so accustomed to Jesse's *cohete* that when a real firecracker went off, I could no longer distinguish between the two. Once during an event, a firecracker went off and my *padrino* and I looked at each other. Then, we both smiled and started laughing. The firecracker interrupted the *jarabe* he and I were dancing. For a second, I thought I had imagined it. The stunned look on my godfather's face told me I did not. "*Hasta parece que andamos en Solaga,*" he commented with a big grin on his face ("It seems like we're in Solaga"). His words echoed my own thoughts. For a brief moment, the firecrackers made me forget I was in someone's backyard in South Central Los Angeles. It *sounded* like we were in Solaga during a patron saint celebration.[26] My immediate thought was that Jesse had made the sound. I looked at Jesse who was neither grinning nor looking around to see people's reactions to his *cohete* as he usually did. It soon dawned on me that the Fourth of July was approaching and firecrackers had been going off for weeks. The firecracker exploding in the exact moment that the *jarabe* reached its peak created the sonic space that transported us all to Solaga. It *felt* like we were in Solaga.

In producing this sound combination, Jesse demonstrates how attuned he is to the soundscape of his parents' hometown. Jesse's whistle is part of a communicative practice that is uniquely shaped by the geographical context from which it emerged. When Jesse re-creates the sound of a *cohete*, or on the odd chance a firecracker is released during a community celebration in Los Angeles, the sound is imbued with more layers of meaning. Through whistling, Jesse engages in a communicative practice entrenched in Solagueño aurality. Whistles abound in Solaga. There are individual, family, and community whistles that alert Solagueños that they are being summoned. There are also whistled phrases produced in lieu of their Zapotec equivalent. The mountainous terrain of the town allows the sounds of whistles to carry over a greater distance than speech. There are also whistles associated with *fiestas*. In the weeks leading up to patron saint celebrations in Solaga, *danzantes* run through their performance with their *maestro* whistling the *son* to which they will eventually dance accompanied by the local or visiting bands. Sometimes these whistles announce danger, like when the *vaqueros* have lost or are about to lose control of a *toro*. Other times, whistles are less serious and are used to teasingly reprimand audio technicians for allowing the *sonido* to go out or a band for missing their turn in the band rotations during the festivities.

Along with music and the sounds of *cohetes*, whistles carry cultural and historical meaning. Zapotec peoples have used autochthonous modalities of communication to their advantage since colonial times. In the Valley of Oaxaca, whistling was used as a strategy of resistance against Spanish colonizers.[27] Porras-Kim notes that because Zapotec is a tonal language, "75 percent of the language can be understood solely via its sound quality and thus emulated by whistling."[28] Whistled speech allowed Zapotecs to make use of what Stó:lō scholar Dylan Robinson terms settlers' tin ear[29] to disguise their conversations. Rather than regarding whistling as a form of communication, Spaniards heard only a musical diversion. Engaging with the Solagueño diaspora's aural practices, including music and sounds, enables us to see how diasporic *wekuell*'s individual and collective experiences and ways of being in the world inform their listening positionality.[30] Their listening positionalities influence how they interact with autochthonous aural practices, including in cases when they may not speak their Indigenous language.

Music as Resistance

As I rushed out of my car into Lorena's backyard with extra *masa* and *tlayudas*[31] for the band's fundraiser, I heard *Solaga USA* playing the first notes to Martin Marcial's *Nho bi che lhue*. Bartolome, a man from the town of San Francisco Yateé who frequents Solagueño events, had a microphone in hand and many of the Solagueños in attendance had pulled out their phones to record his performance. Marcial's songs are rare in that much of the music Serranos play does not have lyrics. Marcial was among the first Serrano singer-songwriters to incorporate lyrics into Oaxacan brass band music in the 1990s. These songs are rooted in Serrano ways of being and knowing the world, including how they understand love, family, and community.[32] Marcial's songs are so popular that *bi wekuell* and Serranos on both sides of the U.S.-Mexico border know the tune to his songs. Thus, while the majority of *Solaga USA* band members did not understand the lyrics of the song, they were able to accompany Bartolome as he sang Marcial's iconic love song.

Marcial's song, set in his native Yateé, is about falling in love with a woman he has never met before. In asking *nho biche lhue*, or "whose child are you?" he attempts to locate her familial and community relations. He goes on to ask her where she lives so that he can visit her and ask for her hand in marriage. He tells the woman how he will raise livestock to take to her home—the traditional dowry in Serrano marriages. Solagueños across generations often perform these marriage rituals, which include dancing by an elder who blesses the newlywed couple and their new home, along with Catholic or civil religious ceremonies in Los Angeles. As with patron saint celebrations, these rituals require the musical accompaniment of the Solagueño youth band who play at Serrano weddings and wedding ceremonies for people from other Oaxacan communities. Through their participation in marriage rituals as *bi wekuell*, youth familiarize themselves with these ancestral practices and some choose to incorporate the Solagueño marriage ritual into their wedding ceremonies.

Music "may be produced under very specific circumstances that grant it particular local significance, but consumed under completely different conditions that in turn help redefine its meaning."[33] For the children of Zapotec immigrants born in diaspora, the first lines of Marcial's song take on a new meaning. Solagueños often attempt to locate the children of Solagueños immigrants visiting from Oaxaca City, Mexico City, and Los Angeles, California, by inquiring about their parentage. With youth responses to *nho bi che nhakbo*, or whose child they are, Solagueños can determine whose kin they are, as well as what their own relation is to diasporic youth. Diasporic returnees may realize that rather than being identified as an individual, in the community they exist within or belong to their families, including their parents, grandparents, and extended family,[34] a different sense of identity than the one they may experience in American settings. Marcial's words remind diasporic youth we no longer live in a place where everyone knows each other. We are the children of displaced people whose community members have trouble locating us as a result of being divided by borders. For youth who do not speak Zapotec, the incomprehensibility of these words is evidence of the realities of living under multiple colonialities.[35] That is, having to contend with legacies of colonization and forced assimilation on our parents' ancestral land but also having to contend with assimilation to the immigrant receiving society in the United States.

In migrating from one settler society to another, Indigenous immigrants must transition into a new society where they continue to be marginalized and racialized as other.[36] Both Mexico and the United States emerge from nation-building projects premised on the idea that the settler is "native" to this land, while perpetuating the myth that the original inhabitants of this land no longer exist.[37] In Mexico's more recent past, *indigenista* policies sought to forcibly incorporate Indigenous people into Mexican society through an eradication of their customs and languages.[38] Schools became sites where Indigenous cultures and languages were deemed useful only as conduits for teaching Indigenous children how to speak European languages.[39] Most Solagueños learned Spanish in primary school and endured physical abuse at the hands of teachers if they spoke Zapotec on school premises.[40] Such mistreatment instills language ideologies that privilege Spanish language use over Indigenous language use even when living in an Indigenous community.[41] Upon emigrating, Solagueños' knowledge of Spanish allowed Solagueño immigrants to communicate with other members of the Latinx immigrant population in the United States. Nevertheless, Indigenous immigrants' physical characteristics and accented Spanish can set them apart from their non-Indigenous counterparts. Informed by their own experiences as Indigenous language speakers and the belief that speaking an Indigenous language could potentially hinder their children's incorporation into American society, Indigenous immigrants may be reluctant to teach their children their native languages. The discrimination Indigenous Latinx immigrants and their children endure in workplaces, schools, and among non-Indigenous Latinx community members may further reinforce these beliefs.[42]

Schools continue to be spaces of exclusion for the children of Indigenous Latinx immigrants.[43] Indigenous Latinx migrant children may be placed into bilingual Spanish/English programs or ESL programs by virtue of their national origin.[44] In conflating national identities with cultural and linguistic identities, school administrators reinforce settler efforts to delegitimize and eliminate Indigenous peoples, cultures, and languages to replace them with their own.[45] As a result, Indigenous Latinx children are instructed in colonial languages (Spanish and English) and thus may experience the U.S. education system as a double colonization.[46] Some Indigenous Latinx families seek out bilingual or dual immersion programs as an investment in their children's futures.[47] In Morales and colleagues' study, Indigenous Latinx children regarded Spanish language proficiency as important for financial, work, and school-related opportunities. For these children, Spanish was transformed from a colonizing or colonial language to a tool for Indigenous *sobrevivencia*. Still, dual immersion programs are often limited to dominant languages, which means that Indigenous language speakers must find "opportunities outside of school to learn, develop, and maintain languages in community settings."[48] Community spaces, like *kermeses* and patron saint celebrations, become sites where Indigenous youth can be exposed to Indigenous languages and aural practices.[49] These moments become an opportunity for youth to engage with their parents and other community members as knowledge bearers. Soundscapes made possible by the existence of the Solagueño youth band produce the context[50] in which diasporic youth can connect with their parents and their ancestors regardless of linguistic ability.[51]

Like Zapotec youth in Martínez and Mesinas's study,[52] diasporic Solagueño youth show various levels of fluency in their community's Indigenous language. While many children of Indigenous Oaxacan immigrants might not be fluent in their parents' Indigenous languages, they have found alternate ways to participate in community life. Nicolas finds that for the Zoochinense community in Los Angeles, language is not a critical component of community members' identity. Rather, their community membership is predicated on their participation in their hometown association, bands, and *danzas*. In the Solagueño case, some Los Angeles–based youth participate in community life as *bi wekuell* and in this capacity contribute to the auditory culture through which Solagueños across generations stay rooted in their community. In doing so, they rely on both new and ancestral ways of showing belonging. *Bi wekuell*'s efforts speak to community-based notions of Indigenous identities that do not equate language use to culture nor take linguistic ability as a marker of Indigenous authenticity or community membership.[53]

While they may be unable to understand Martin Marcial's lyrics, the members of *Solaga USA* have grown up hearing his songs. So much so that when Bartolome or even Martin Marcial show up to their events and sing, youth are able to play for them without necessarily understanding the lyrics of these Zapotec songs. Their immersion in and contribution to Serrano auditory culture allows them to connect their place of settlement with their place of origin, as well as index belonging to their Indigenous community.[54] In this way, Indigenous youth both demonstrate that language loss does not signal loss of identity and is not a criterion through which Indigenous individual identity or cultural authenticity can be assessed.[55]

Instead of listening with a tin ear, we must turn our attention to the aural modalities of communication in Indigenous communities through which community members across generations rely. When Zapotec songs are performed at Solagueño events, there is no attempt at translation. Rather, Serranos across generations and linguistic ability come together in the act of listening.[56] In not distinguishing between music and language, Serranos engage language and music as part of a semiotic field of meaning that decenters the importance of text as the object of analysis.[57] Settler listening logics prioritize capturing "the content of what is spoken, or the 'fact' of musical form and structure ... over the affective feel, timbre, touch, and texture of sound."[58] By attending to the way music and sounds make us *feel* and the memories the aural evokes, as Matias suggests, we engage in a politics of listening more attuned to Indigenous epistemologies and sensory logics.[59]

Bartolome, Martin Marcial, and other *bene wekuell* are key to maintaining connections across borders. The bodies of musicians, Chávez argues, bear traces of the places they have known and alter the places where they have been, allowing musicians to move physically across distances and to move people emotionally, thereby solidifying connections across borders.[60] In this way, individuals can use music to locate themselves in different geographies at the same time. *Bene wekuell* not only bear the traces of the places where they have been, but like Jesse use their musical ability to transport Solagueños to their homeland by appealing to their aural sensibilities. *Bene wekuell* are also critical to the deterritorialization and reterritorialization of Oaxacan communal practices. Key to the reterritorialization of musical practices, Madrid argues, is the appropriation of hegemonic symbols and their reconfiguration to the needs of the community.[61] Thus, while European colonizers appropriated Indigenous dance and musical practices in their efforts to colonize and evangelize Indigenous populations, Indigenous peoples have reappropriated these practices and embedded within them the values of *comunalidad* and the importance of living in community.[62] While Payan Ramirez demonstrates how young musicians enact *comunalidad* in an *escoleta* in Oaxaca,[63] I demonstrate that *bene wekuell's* practices allow community members (musicians and nonmusicians alike) to enact, model, and impart these values to children and youth born away from the Indigenous homeland. To do this, I demonstrate the importance of the space the Solagueño youth band creates as a site of learning and belonging. Like the aural practices with which diasporic youth engage, this learning falls outside of Western pedagogical practices and spaces and instead relies on Indigenous knowledge systems and approaches to learning in community.

La kermés: Modeling Collective Participation

I arrived at Lorena's home in Mid-City Los Angeles a little before 10 a.m. to help with the *kermés*. Lorena's backyard has become a center for Solagueño social gatherings, particularly those hosted by the Solagueño youth band. Band members' fathers were unloading tables and chairs from a van. I greeted the men who were gathered in the backyard and headed to Lorena's kitchen, where women were preparing food. Inside, I found my Tía Mariana and the mothers of other band members slicing cabbage that would be used as a topping for the *tlayudas* they were going to sell at the fundraiser. Lorena offered me a cup of *café de Solaga* and bread. While I had already eaten breakfast, I knew I could not refuse. Both in Los Angeles and Solaga, it is rude to refuse food that someone offers you upon entering their home. While I ate, the women began setting up outside. Once I was done, I went outside to inquire how I could help. One of the women asked me to put tablecloths on the tables where guests would sit. As I began to cut table-length pieces from the table cover roll, Sebastian, a second-generation band member, arrived with an Asian-American friend. Since the food was not ready, the women asked Sebastian and his friend to help me. Sebastian's friend, Henry, and I cut pieces from the roll as Sebastian taped the tablecloths to the bottom of each table. By the time we were done, the women had finished setting up and were at their assigned food stations, which included a *tlayuda* station, a *champurrado* and coffee station, a *quesadilla* station, and a station selling *tortillas con rellena* and *empanadas*. The men were assigned to the bar area, where they collected donations and sold the tickets people would use to pay for their food, as well as alcoholic and non-alcoholic beverages.

Eventually, Solagueños and *paisanos* from surrounding towns in the Sierra Juarez started arriving for the *kermés*. Some came with their entire families, while others came during their lunch break to pick up food for themselves and their coworkers or for Solagueños they knew who worked near them. I took orders for the women in charge of the *quesadilla* station for most of the day and served individuals who ordered from our station, occasionally helping the women at other stations. Band members did not arrive until close to 1 p.m., an hour before they were set to play. The band's performance at fundraisers typically draws larger crowds, so band members' arrival meant that the latter half of the day was busier—so much so that various stations began running out of food items like *masa* and *tlayudas*, which I was sent out to procure.

Fundraisers are held to raise money to rent the band's practice space, which is also funded by the band's performances at events like weddings and quinceañeras. *Kermeses* are also organized to fundraise for community projects in the hometown, including purchasing instruments for children in the hometown's youth band. The parents of band members take care of the logistics of the fundraisers, including preparing food at home and at the *kermés*, as well as purchasing many of the items necessary for the fundraisers.

While the parents of band members do much of the organizing for band-sponsored patron saint celebrations and fundraisers, community members also participate in these events. These contributions take many forms, from helping in the execution of the fundraiser by cooking or setting up, to donating items, to traveling across Los Angeles during a lunch break to contribute to the fundraiser. Underlying these actions are notions of belonging based on individuals' contributions to collective community life.[64] While Solagueños may have been socialized in these practices in their hometown,[65] they continue these practices in diaspora and express their willingness to be recognized as part of the collective.[66] Diasporic Zapotec parents who are highly involved in their hometown encourage their children to become involved in traditional dances and brass bands so they, too, can connect with family and friends and learn about their customs and traditions.[67] Among Solagueños, parental involvement in *Solaga USA* events allows immigrants to build and maintain ties between Solaga and Oaxacan communities in Los Angeles, while transmitting their ancestral values and modeling collective participation as practiced in their hometown.

Indigenous peoples transmit their ways of knowing and being to the next generation through modeling, practice, and animation of everyday familial and community practices.[68] Through *comunalidad*, Solagueños have a means through which they can participate in community life and ensure the survival of their way of life. Through their participation in collective practices across their lifetime, Solagueños acquire Indigenous knowings and "responsibilities that model competent and respectful behavior toward others and the natural world and form part of families' and communities' funds of knowledge and community cultural wealth."[69] Importantly, this learning occurs through observing and participating in family and community activities as children and youth.[70] *Solaga USA* creates the sites in which displaced Solagueños can enact *comunalidad* through *fiestas* and model these practices for their children. In staging and participating in community events, Solagueño immigrants act on a sense of responsibility for their *pueblo* and demonstrate their willingness to continue being part of the community[71] in diaspora. This enactment of *comunalidad* allows Solagueños to fulfill an obligation to the community and show belonging to the collective.[72] Instilling this ethic in the next generation is integral for the social reproduction of Indigenous communal life. While these practices were modeled for Solagueños as children in their hometown, they continue to embrace and engage in these practices and allow their children to learn from them and choose whether they too will engage in *comunalidad*. As Nicolas's work among Zoochinenses demonstrates, many Zapotecs born in diaspora choose to maintain these practices.[73]

While I went to the *kermés* with the intent to help, Sebastian and Henry showed up to purchase food. Having arrived a little too early and with setup still pending, Sebastian and his friend were quickly recruited to help in preparations for the *kermés*. As a Solagueño, Sebastian was expected to contribute to the success of the *kermés*. This expectation stems from the way of life that *comunalidad* instills in Indigenous Oaxacans, who are expected to contribute to their community through participating in communal life, in this case the organization of a *fiesta. Fiestas* fall under what Mendoza Zuany categorizes as the social sphere of *comunalidad* or what Martínez Luna calls the philosophy of *goce* (enjoyment) within *comunalidad*.[74] These concepts recognize the labor that goes into organizing community celebrations, as well as the joy and fulfillment community members receive from the outcome of their shared labor—*fiestas* through which they can support their community. While his contribution is usually his musicianship, Sebastian's premature arrival to share a meal with a friend afforded him the additional opportunity to contribute in the preparations for the event. Furthermore, their early arrival also provided Sebastian's friend, Henry, the chance to participate in communal life. Because everyone can partake in *comunalidad* regardless of birthplace and language,[75] Henry's aid in the staging of the *kermés* was an entrée into Solagueño communal life. A sustained engagement in Solagueño collective practices would most likely bring him into the community, since community members would recognize his contributions to the community as an expression of belonging.

Ultimately, the success of a Solagueño *kermés* falls on the shoulders of the Solagueño youth band since they are the focal point of this event. While this fundraiser was an all-day event, the band's presence drew the biggest crowd. Their appearance guaranteed community members could come together to enjoy an afternoon of listening and dancing to music from their region, while supporting the youth band. The band's music sometimes draws neighbors and strangers in the area who wander into Lorena's backyard to investigate what all the commotion is about. Because music follows Serranos, they are not only able to enact collective participation to stage successful fundraising events to help their community at home and abroad, but are also able to draw non-Solagueños to their cause. Like brass bands in Oaxaca, the Solagueño youth band's commitment to their community does critical work that allows the Solagueño community to foster relations with other Indigenous communities, while creating spaces where the next generation can learn and draw on communal values.

Conclusion

Oaxacan aural practices have not only become an identifier of Oaxacans and their culture in diaspora, but also allow diasporic Solagueño youth to engage with the auditory cultural practices of their *pueblo*. In addition to music, this auditory culture includes sounds that Serranos across time, space, and generation identify with their homeland. The sonic space *bene wekuell* create reminds us not only of where we come from but who we are and how we are in relation with each other. Oaxacan *wekuell* in Mexico and the United States use the means through which their ancestors were colonized to resist ongoing settler colonial processes and transmit their ancestral values and way of life away from their places of origin. In doing so, Indigenous immigrants ensure the survival of their collective identities while centering their ways of knowing and being in the world. These practices are necessary as Indigenous immigrants and their children contend with assaults to their Indigenous identities by some members of the Latinx population and increasing hostility toward immigrant communities in the United States.

Youth musicians' auditory practices rely on the sensorial experiences of the ancestral homeland they can evoke through sound in order to create a space through which they can mediate displacement. For many Solagueños, their legal status prevents them from returning to their hometown. Nevertheless, they are able to experiences the sounds of Solaga through *Solaga USA*'s musicianship. While living in diaspora, these musicians use autochthonous modalities of communication to construct their social world. In doing so, they are not only able to demonstrate belonging to community—despite being born abroad or not speaking their Indigenous language—but also create the space in which Solagueños in diaspora can practice and teach their children how to live in community.

Conclusion

IN THE SUMMER OF 2022, Serranos in Oaxaca City organized a *calenda* to protest the Sierra Norte region's exclusion from the state-sponsored Guelaguetza, a festival that showcases music and dance traditions from the Oaxaca's eight regions. This *calenda* was spearheaded by the Serrano Zapotec communities of Betaza and Yalalag, who along with their Oaxaca City–based bands marched and danced through the city's central streets. Music followed Serranos to Oaxaca City as it later did with Serranos in Los Angeles, California. My cousin Isaac advertised the *calenda* on his social media and we made plans to meet at the protest. As we marched between Betaza and Yalalag's delegations, I saw a sign protesting this perceived slight from festival organizers: We unite as Oaxacans in outrage that the Sierra [Norte] region, birthplace of Licenciado Benito Juarez Garcia, is not a part of the Guelaguetza's "Lunes del Cerro." While Oaxacans have critiqued the government's cooptation and commodification of Zapotec *guelaguetza* (*gozona*) traditions,[1] Betazeños, Yalaltecos, and the Serranos who joined in their protest were outraged that that year's festival did not include the Sierra Juarez region.

At the end of the underwhelming, yet packed official Guelaguetza *calenda* one day earlier, the omission of a Serrano delegation, my cousins pointed out, made the parade less enjoyable. Had they been there with a delegation from Solaga as they had in years past, they assured me, they would have put on a show. In response to the state's attempted erasure, though, Serranos then organized their own *calenda* to display the rich dance and musical traditions from the birthplace of Mexico's only Indigenous president, Benito Juarez. Together, this event and the protest sign demonstrate the pride diasporic Serranos feel in their communal histories and identities, including their distinct regional and town-specific identities and cultural practices. The Serrano *calenda* foreshadowed the Oaxacan protests that would erupt in Los Angeles months later when a Mexican-origin politician disparaged the Oaxacan community based on their Indigenous phenotype. Most notably, Oaxacan Angelenos responded to this affront by engaging in Serrano soundscapes and asserting the same communal identities their Oaxaca City counterparts had asserted. Some of these identities, I learned, have different meanings across borders.

Diasporic Solagueños across Settler States

"*¿Cuándo llegaron de su ... pueblo? ¿O cómo se dice?*"[2] Enrique, my cousin Isaac's friend, hesitated as he finished his statement. He stared at us trying to gauge if he had said something offensive. "*Sí. Pueblo. Se dice pueblo,*"[3] another cousin responded, slightly annoyed. In that moment, I was sure Enrique was going to refer to Solaga, our *pueblo*, as a *pueblucho* or *pueblito*.[4] Despite joining Isaac for the Serrano *calenda*, Enrique did not seem to know what to do with our presence outside of our *pueblo* or how to refer to our hometown without potentially offending us by acknowledging our origins in an Indigenous community. Even in a city that flourishes through the commodification of Oaxaca's Indigenous communities and cultures, including through the Guelaguetza festival, as Indigenous peoples we did not belong in Oaxaca City. Unbeknownst to Enrique, the cousins that accompanied me had long lived in the city and while I *had* just arrived in Oaxaca City from Solaga, I was born in the urban metropolis of Los Angeles, California. That soon became the topic of conversation at the dinner table.

As we waited for our food, Isaac explained to his friend, "There was a generation that had to migrate to the United States from our *pueblo*. That's why my cousin was born in *el gabacho,*"[5] Isaac shared with Enrique, who like him was born in Oaxaca City. It was the first time I heard someone have to articulate an experience that was so obvious to Solagueños: there was a generation of community members that *had* to migrate to the United States from our *pueblo*. Indeed, all of the Solagueños at the table had family members who had migrated to Los Angeles during the time period Isaac referenced. While Isaac did not elaborate on the circumstances leading to Solagueño emigration, he communicated that my parents' generation had no other choice but to leave their hometown and head to Los Angeles. In two sentences, Isaac summarized how I—and the larger Solagueño community in Los Angeles—came to exist. Isaac then shared that I was a *doctora en antropología*. "My cousin speaks Zapotec, English, and Spanish," my cousin continued, bragging as if my doctorate explained my linguistic ability. Enrique, however, was most impressed at my English-speaking ability. At Isaac's encouragement, I shared with Enrique my research on how the children of Solagueño immigrants formed their identities in Los Angeles.

Isaac, who had traveled to the United States as part of an academic exchange program, then explained to Enrique that Oaxacans experience racism in the United States. "It's from Americans and Mexicans," I interjected, recalling the weird feeling I had after Enrique's hesitation earlier. "Why would other Mexicans discriminate against Oaxacans?" Enrique wondered in disbelief. "Because we're Indigenous," I responded. "They see all Oaxacans as Indigenous," I added, realizing that "Oaxacan" had become synonymous with "Indigenous" in diaspora and that the Oaxacan that sat across from me likely saw himself as different from the Indigenous people sitting around the table. I had been so enmeshed in the Solagueño diaspora in Los Angeles, both as a community member and as a researcher, that I had given little thought to the experiences of diasporic Solagueños in Oaxaca City and Mexico City.[6] While I had long considered state-sponsored racism as a factor that contributed to Solagueño emigration, this interaction showed me that one only had to travel four hours away from our hometown to encounter interpersonal anti-Indigenous prejudice from people Solagueños considered friends and community members. While not as overt as the experiences of discrimination diasporic Solagueños in Los Angeles encountered—being called "little Indians" or "Oaxaquitas" by "friends" and elected officials alike—this interaction demonstrated the continued salience of racial stereotypes and hierarchies that affect the lives of Indigenous peoples in their home state, as well as throughout Latin America and in the United States.

In October 2022, three months after the Serrano *calenda* in Oaxaca City, headline news broke—leaked audio recordings featured Latinx Los Angeles City Council members disparaging Indigenous and Black Angelenos, among other groups. Referring to Oaxacans living in Koreatown, Nury Martinez remarked, "I don't know where these people are from. Like I don't know what village they came out of, how they got here. But ... ¡*'Tan feos!*"[7] As *The Children of Solaga* demonstrates, the racial tropes Nury Martinez invoked are not new. They echo the racial descriptors Rebecca's high school peers employed in the early 2000s to ascertain if someone was Oaxacan: "If they are short, dark, and ugly, they are from Oaxaca." While the leaked audio was certainly triggering for the Oaxacan community of Los Angeles, some Oaxacans were more insulted that Martinez was so dismissive of their *pueblos*. Community members' protest signs responded to Martinez's affront with the names of the communities from which they are descended. "Proudly representing San Baltazar Yatzachi El Bajo y Santa Maria Xochixtepec Sierra Juarez," one sign read. For people whose identity is rooted in collective societies, Martinez's words were more injurious because she had insulted their *pueblos*.

The Oaxacan response to the Los Angeles City Council leak was also notable in the role that Indigenous practices of belonging played during these protests. Indigenous Oaxacans not only asserted their communal identities in the face of racism from their co-national, Nury Martinez; they responded to this racist incident with their brass bands and their *sones* and *jarabes*. Like Serranos in Oaxaca City, diasporic Indigenous Oaxacans in Los Angeles used communal practices that settlers have read as apolitical musical diversions to assert their distinct identities. As *The Children of Solaga* demonstrates, music and dance are part of Solagueño (and more broadly Serrano) practices of belonging and this remains the case across borders. Oaxacan brass bands in Los Angeles keep diasporic

Indigenous Oaxacans and their U.S.-born or -raised children connected to their communities of origin and allow us to mediate displacement and alienation in our new homes. As a result of these diasporic practices, rather than feeling ashamed of their *pueblos* or their Indigenous features, Oaxacans used the aural practices that have come to distinguish Oaxacans from other groups in Los Angeles to uphold the very identities for which they were belittled. While Matias may have prematurely called his high school "Home of the Oaxacans," the fact that he had the confidence to do so demonstrates that Indigenous children and youth have grown up in spaces across Los Angeles where their Indigenous communal identities and practices are appreciated and even uplifted. Throughout *The Children of Solaga*, I consider how exclusion drives Indigenous children and youth's continued involvement and investment in their community of origin. When faced with racial discrimination, diasporic Oaxacans now respond with the communal joy they experience though their communal identities and practices. Still, the Oaxacan community in Los Angeles is unique. As the main destination for Oaxacan immigrants, Los Angeles may be as close to "home" as Indigenous Oaxacans can get in diaspora. This, however, may not be the case for all diasporic Indigenous Latinx children and youth.

On Displacement and Loss

As an Indigenous Latinx professor who teaches about and researches Indigenous migration, displacement, and identity formation, I often come into contact with students who also have origins in Indigenous communities in Latin America. One of the concerns I often hear from Indigenous Latinx students is, "What's going to happen?" They are justifiably scared that because they are not connected to their Indigenous communities or do not speak their Indigenous language, their Indigenous cultures and identities will be lost. Like Kevin, who blamed himself for his parents' unauthorized presence in the United States rather than immigration policies that privilege select groups of people for authorized migration, these students blame themselves for the loss of their Indigenous cultures, languages, and identities rather than the settler ideologies and structures that forcibly assimilate Indigenous peoples and deny them the right to remain in their communities of origin.

The sense of loss the children of Indigenous immigrants feel usually stems from the idea that because they live outside of their homeland, they are "less Indigenous." Ultimately, as the child of Indigenous immigrants, I share the concerns of children of Indigenous immigrants about the future because I too do not know what the future holds for our homelands and for the communities we have created in diaspora. My only reassurance to them is that despite colonization and over five hundred years of attempts to eradicate our cultures and assimilate us into Latin American and American settler states, we are still here. I remind students that culture is always changing and so too is what it means to be Indigenous. Change is inevitable for people like our parents who were displaced from their Indigenous communities, as well as for their children who grow up away from these communities and navigate multiple structures that stigmatize and try to eradicate their cultures and identities.

Our communities have long been portrayed as in danger of disappearing. This myth, Kauanui argues, is part of the settler colonial project that seeks to dispossess Indigenous peoples from their lands and refute their claims to land and rights.[8] Indeed, anthropology, the discipline in which I am trained, played a big role in perpetuating the myth of the inevitable demise of Indigenous peoples.[9] So too did settler retellings of history, or what Jean O'Brien terms "firsting and lasting."[10] Using local histories from nineteenth-century New England, O'Brien demonstrates how Anglo settlers memorialized Indigenous peoples, who still lived among them, and chronicled their extinction. By erasing contemporary Indigenous peoples or denying their Indigeneity on the grounds of racial purity, Anglo settlers established their region as the cradle of the Anglo-Saxon nation and perpetuated the myth of Indigenous extinction.

Science, Kim TallBear argues, is now also being used to similar ends. TallBear writes about the danger of the use of "Native American DNA" as part of the process of tribal enrollment. By treating Indigenous groups as biological or population-based genetic samples, scientists may undermine Indigenous articulations of Indigeneity or the ways in which Indigenous peoples conceptualize biological and cultural kinship and determine belonging.[11] Genomic technologies, considered unbiased because they are "scientific," can then be used by settler states whose nation-building projects rely on the elimination of the native.

While much of this work is based on the experiences of Indigenous groups in North America, these ideas extend to Indigenous people from Latin America. In fact, American racial ideologies have shaped Latin American ideas about race. The theory of *mestizaje* emerged in the early twentieth century as a response to American imperialist ideas about the racial inferiority of Latin Americans.[12] Americans believed Latin America's large multiracial population made them incapable of governing themselves. Instead, Mexican philosopher José Vasconcelos posited that *mestizaje* was "thoroughly desirable."[13] Juliet Hooker argues that Vasconcelos's theorization of *mestizaje* conflated racial mixture with racial egalitarianism in its proposition that cultural and biological mixture brought about by colonization produced mixed, homogenous national populations who now lived in countries with no racial stratification or discrimination. Although the valorization of *mestizaje* improved the status of Latin Americans of mixed origin, the myth of *mestizaje* has since been criticized for promoting racism and the historical erasure of Indigenous and Afro-descendant peoples.[14] Yomaira Figueroa-Vásquez notes how *mestizaje* "relegates both Blackness and Indigeneity to backwards moves within national imaginaries and nation-building projects that seek to move towards whiteness."[15] The continued use of *indio* as a derogatory, racial slur to connote backwardness, anti-progress, and retrogradation[16] demonstrates that this remains true.

In their attempts to completely eradicate their Indigenous populations, Latin American settler states have institutionalized policies that promote assimilation into the national fold. Indeed, Vasconcelos's appointment as minister of education of Mexico allowed him to build schools and institutions to promote his theory of *mestizaje* and institutionalize assimilationist policies.[17] For Solagueños and other Indigenous children, schools became sites where teachers used corporal punishment to discourage children from speaking their Indigenous language.[18] Language ideologies that privilege European over Indigenous languages persist among Solagueños in the hometown and in the diaspora. Thus, when students blame themselves for their lack of proficiency in their Indigenous language, I point them toward the anti-Indigenous context in which their parents were likely raised and to which they migrated; these factors may have made parents reluctant to teach their children their native languages.[19] Diasporic Indigenous children and youth may find they no longer possess the linguistic, biological, or physical characteristics that have become associated with Indigeneity,[20] further exacerbating their sense of loss.

Displacement further exacerbates the loss associated with Indigenous peoples' experiences. In their homelands, from an early age Indigenous people are inculcated with messages that they and their cultures are to blame for the poverty in which they likely grow up. Upon arriving in the United States, moreover, they soon learn that English is now the language of power and are less likely to teach their children their Indigenous languages or openly discuss their Indigenous background. By the time their children take my classes on migration or Indigeneity, the children of Indigenous immigrants have come to believe that because they do not speak an Indigenous language or live in their homeland, they are complicit in the loss of their culture. Instead, as I do in *The Children of Solaga*, the materials in my classes direct their attention to the structural forces that not only led our parents to migrate, but also inform how we as diasporic Indigenous people form our identities away from our ancestral homelands.

Sometimes I dream about the life I would have had if I had not been born *en el gabacho*. Had my parents not had to leave their hometown. Admittedly, these thoughts are fantastical and do not take into account the poverty many Solagueños still live in and which my ancestors fled. I also remind myself that being born and educated in diaspora has given me both the distance and tools to reflect on and appreciate the different ways of being, knowing, and belonging that allow us as Solagueños to find communal joy in our ancestral practices and ways of life. I find joy in knowing that many Los Angeles–born Oaxacan children and youth do not know a world without our aural traditions or where they as *wekuell* and border crossers are central to the reproduction of our communal life. While we do not know a world outside of the colonial legacies we inherited and the settler structures that continue to influence our lives, the community we have created in Los Angeles allows us to *feel* like we are home in places where we are meant to feel unwanted.

GLOSSARY

Dixa xhon	English
Bi che	The child of
Bi wekuell	Musician or a group of musicians
Bene wekuell	Musicians
Bi walhall	Local person or a group of local people
Bene walhall	Local people
Da walhall	Local object
Gwzon	Zapotec system of reciprocity or mutual aid; part of the second pillar of *comunalidad*
Weya'	Dancer
Xhesua	The grandchild of
Yell	Community

Spanish	English
Calenda	Dance and music procession that announces the beginning of patron saint celebrations; these parades are now also held outside of religious contexts
Casa de la comisión de festejos	Communal building where community members stop during *calendas* and visitors are fed during patron saint celebrations in Solaga
Chisme	Gossip
Comisión de festejos	Committee in charge of organizing patron saint celebrations

Spanish	English
Comunalidad	A set of practices and way of knowing and being in the world through which Indigenous Oaxacans demonstrate belonging to their community
Convivencia	The practice of living and engaging with people and place through which Indigenous peoples form and cultivate bonds with their *pueblo* and come to belong to their community
Convivir	To live in and engage with
Danzas	Choreographed dances performed during patron saint celebrations
Danzantes	Dancers
El goce comunal	Communal joy; feeling of communal joy community members reap from their contributions to and participation in communal life; the fourth pillar of *comunalidad*
Escoleta	Rehearsal space for Solagueño bands in Mexico and the United States
Fiestas	Patron saint celebrations
Gozona	Zapotec system of reciprocity or mutual aid; part of the second pillar of comunalidad
Jaripeo	Bull riding
Kermés	Fundraiser
Mayordomo/a	Sponsor of an event, prize, or patron saint celebration
Mayordomía	Sponsorship of an event, prize, or patron saint celebration
Mestizo	A person of mixed Indigenous and Spanish ancestry
Misas oaxaqueñas	Catholic Mass service with Oaxacan band accompaniment
Paisano(s)	Local person or people; the Spanish equivalent of *bene* or *bi walhall*
Promesa	A sacred vow made to a Catholic saint in exchange for their help
Pueblo	An Indigenous community; people from the community

Spanish	English
Recua	An event during patron saint celebrations in which community members dance and hand out treats, toys, and household items to locals and visitors
Serrano(s)	Person or people from Oaxaca's Sierra Juarez or Sierra Norte region
Sones y jarabes	Musical pieces performed by Oaxacan brass bands
Tequio	Communal labor; part of the second pillar of comunalidad
Usos y costumbres	Local governance based on an Indigenous community's customary practices

NOTES

Introduction

    1. As Rubén Rumbaut ("Immigration, Incorporation, and Generational Cohorts in Historical Contexts") notes, "International migration is a powerful and transformative force, producing profound social changes not only in the sending and receiving societies, but, above all, among the immigrants themselves and their descendants" (53). Thus, I employ migration scholars' use of immigrant generations, including first, 1.5, and second. I do this not to indicate how far removed Solagueños are from original migrations or the conditions that produced these migrations, as scholars originally intended, but because they are indicative of more than nascency. For a community whose first-generation immigrant population likely migrated without authorization, immigrant generation is linked to citizenship and the ability to move freely across borders.

    2. *The Children of Solaga* employs the concept of diaspora to stress the diasporic nature of Solagueño life. Diaspora has been defined as "a transnational community whose members (or their ancestors) emigrated or were dispersed from their original homeland but remain oriented to it and preserve a group identity" (Grossman, "Toward a Definition of Diaspora," 1267). In referring to the Solagueño diaspora, I acknowledge that some Solagueños, their children, and their grandchildren have lived outside of their Indigenous homeland for several generations. Solagueños live in Oaxaca City, Mexico City, and Los Angeles, California, yet remain oriented to their homeland. Having community members who live in diaspora informs how the community has come to determine belonging and how diasporic Solagueños attempt to build and maintain ties to their homeland. Importantly, this orientation to homeland is grounded in Serrano ways of being and knowing the world, and the preservation of communal identities that are re-created and created in diaspora.

3. Stephen, "Indigenous Transborder Citizenship," 134.

4. I use diasporic Solagueños to identify Solagueños living away of their homeland regardless of immigrant generation. I use diasporic Solagueño children and youth to identify the children of Solagueño immigrants who grow up or are born away from their ancestral homeland.

5. Martínez Luna, *Comunalidad y desarrollo.*

6. Solagueños' Zapotec last names may recognize the ancestral origins of a family (like my father's), may be the Zapotec surname of a Solagueño family (like my maternal grandfather's and my mother's), reflect the Zapotec version of a Spanish surname (like my maternal grandmother's), or may be based on one's or an ancestor's nickname.

7. When I was a child, relatives and community members often gifted me with fruit and eggs that were *da walhall,* or grown or produced in Solaga. In emphasizing that they were *da walhall,* gift givers stressed that their gifts were humble, yet precious because they were local to the community.

8. Hurtado, *Intersectional Chicana Feminisms.*

9. Archuleta, "I Give You Back."

10. Anzaldúa, *Making Face, Making Soul/Haciendo Caras;* Hurtado, *Intersectional Chicana Feminisms;* Simpson, *Mohawk Interruptus.*

11. Shkodriani and Gibbons, "Individualism and Collectivism among University Students in Mexico and the United States," 766.

12. Diaz-Loving and Draguns, "Culture, Meaning, and Personality in Mexico and in the United States." These different understandings of the self reflect Western and Indigenous ways of understand the world, including thinking of the world from the perspective of the individual and thinking about the world from a collective perspective (Martínez Luna, "Conocimiento y comunalidad").

13. Huang et al., "Transnational Leisure Experience of Second-generation Immigrants."

14. Individuals born abroad and brought to the United States as children.

15. Tsuda, "Is Native Anthropology Really Possible?"

16. Solagueños and people from neighboring communities use *Zoolaga* to refer to Solaga when conversing with Zapotec speakers. However, Solagueños and Serranos usually refer to the community and community members as Solaga and Solagueños, respectively. As a result, I use Solaga throughout this text.

17. "San Andrés Solaga," n.d., *Gobierno de Mexico,* https://www.economia. gob.mx/datamexico/es/profile/geo/san-andres-solaga#population-and-housing.

18. United States Census Bureau, *Los Angeles city, California,* Data.Census. Gov, https://www.census.gov/quickfacts/fact/table/losangelescitycalifornia/ PST045222 (February 23, 2024).

19. Kummels, *Indigeneity in Real Time.*

20. Celis et al. *San Andrés Solaga: Lugar de hojas regadas.*

21. Sánchez and Martínez, my grandfather's surnames, are common among Yojoveños. I often try to bond with Yojoveños who share my last name and suggest we might be related because my grandfather was born there. Their response is always the same: they did not know my grandfather and we are not related. Instead, they stress my connection to my mother's sister, a Solagueña who married a Yojoveño, and to Solaga.

22. If I formed a sustained relationship with Yojovi and actively participated in Yojoveño communal life, I could be reincorporated into Yojovi just like my ancestors were incorporated into Solaga through their participation in communal institutions.

23. I would even argue my involvement in Solagueño communal life began during my first trip to Solaga as my mother modeled what it is like to participate in communal life through participation in patron saint celebrations.

24. Kresge, "Indigenous Oaxacan Communities in California: An Overview."

25. While Solaga is a Zapotec community, people from Zapotec and Mixes communities have settled in the town.

26. Saldívar and Walsh, "Racial and Ethnic Identities in Mexican Statistics."

27. Welchman Gegeo, "Cultural Rupture and Indigeneity"; Aikau, "Indigeneity in the Diaspora"; Blackwell, Boj Lopez, and Urrieta, "Critical Latinx Indigeneities."

28. Figueroa-Vásquez, *Decolonizing Diasporas*, 9. The word *indio* continues to be used as a derogatory slur, since it carries connotations of backwardness, anti-progress, and retrogradation (Friedlander, "The Secularization of the Cargo System"; Kearney, "Transnational Oaxacan Indigenous Identity"; Wilson, "Cultural Politics of Race and Ethnicity"). Along with previous research, I found that negative connotations associated with people of Indigenous origin carry over to the United States, where some *mestizo* immigrants and their children continue to discriminate against other immigrants because of their Indigenous origin (Blackwell, Boj Lopez, and Urrieta, "Critical Latinx Indigeneities"; Kearney, "Transnational Oaxacan Indigenous Identity"; Ortiz and Pombo, "Indigenous Migration in Mexico and Central America Interethnic Relations and Identity Transformations"; Stephen, *Transborder Lives*).

29. Figueroa-Vásquez, *Decolonizing Diasporas*, 9.

30. Tuhiwai Smith, "The Native and the Neoliberal Down Under."

31. Leo Chavez, *Covering Immigration*, 295.

32. Fitzpatrick, "We know what it is when you do not ask us," 10.

33. Gamio, *Forjando Patria.*

34. Ortiz Elizondo and Hernández Castillo, "Constitutional Amendments and New Imaginings of the Nation," 60.

35. Holmes, *Fresh Fruit, Broken Bodies*; Kearney, "Transnational Oaxacan Indigenous Identity."

36. Barillas-Chón, "Oaxaqueño/a Students' (Un)Welcoming High School Experiences"; Ruiz and Barajas, "Multiple Perspectives on the Schooling of Mexican Indigenous Students in the US"; Urrieta, "Las identidades también lloran/Identities Also Cry."

37. Stephen, *Transborder Lives*.

38. Dolores Inés Casillas, *Sounds of Belonging*.

39. Leo Chavez, *The Latino Threat*.

40. Importantly, scholars and activists have challenged the use of "illegal" in public discourse by pointing toward the role of the U.S. state in the production of illegality. Revisions to immigration law, for example, have diminished the possibilities for Mexicans to migrate to the U.S. legally "and thus played an instrumental role in the production of a legally vulnerable undocumented workforce of 'illegal aliens'" (De Genova, "The Legal Production of Mexican/Migrant 'Illegality,'" 161).

41. Chavez, *The Latino Threat*.

42. Clifford, "Diasporas"; Sanchez, "Racial and Structural Discrimination toward the Children of Indigenous Mexican Immigrants."

43. Blackwell, Boj Lopez, and Urrieta, "Critical Latinx Indigeneities."

44. Blackwell, Boj Lopez, and Urrieta, "Critical Latinx Indigeneities"; Boj Lopez, "Mobile Archives of Indigeneity"; Speed, "States of Violence: Indigenous Women Migrants in the Era of Neoliberal Multicriminalism."

45. Urrieta, Mesinas, and Martínez, "Critical Latinx Indigeneities and Education," 7; see also Urrieta, "Diasporic Community Smartness."

46. Alberto, "Coming Out as Indian"; Boj Lopez, "Mobile Archives of Indigeneity"; Nicolas, "Soy de Zoochina: Zapotecs across Generations"; Sánchez-López, "Learning from the *paisanos*"; Urrieta, "Identity, Violence, and Authenticity."

47. Blackwell, Boj Lopez, and Urrieta, "Critical Latinx Indigeneities," 130.

48. Nicolas, "Soy de Zoochina: Zapotecs across Generations."

49. Boj Lopez, "Mobile Archives of Indigeneity."

50. Blackwell, Boj Lopez, and Urrieta, "Critical Latinx Indigeneities"; Speed, *Incarcerated Stories*.

51. Wolfe, "Settler Colonialism and the Elimination of the Native"; Smithers, "What Is an Indian?"; Calderón, "Uncovering Settler Grammars in Curriculum"; O'Brien, *Firsting and Lasting*.

52. Wolfe, "Settler Colonialism and the Elimination of the Native," 388.

53. Speed, *Incarcerated Stories*.

54. Blackwell, Boj Lopez, and Urrieta, "Critical Latinx Indigeneities"; Speed, *Incarcerated Stories*.

55. Blackwell, Boj Lopez, and Urrieta, "Critical Latinx Indigeneities."

56. Heidbrink, *Migranthood*; Speed, *Incarcerated Stories.*

57. Speed, *Incarcerated Stories.*

58. Fox and Rivera-Salgado, "Building Civil Society among Indigenous Migrants"; Blackwell et al., "Critical Latinx Indigeneities"; Gegeo, "Cultural Rupture and Indigeneity."

59. Rivera-Salgado, "Transnational Indigenous Communities: The Intellectual Legacy of Michael Kearney."

60. Massey et al., *Return to Aztlan.*

61. Cardoso, *Mexican Emigration to the United States 1897–1931*; Rivera-Salgado, "Transnational Indigenous Communities: The Intellectual Legacy of Michael Kearney."

62. Loza, *Defiant Braceros.*

63. Inda, *Targeting Immigrants.*

64. Massey et al., *Return to Aztlan.*

65. Massey, Durand, and Malone, *Beyond Smoke and Mirrors.*

66. Cohen, "Transnational Migration in Rural Oaxaca, Mexico: Dependency, Development, and the Household."

67. Ortiz and Pombo, "Indigenous Migration in Mexico and Central America Interethnic Relations and Identity Transformations."

68. Cohen, "Transnational Migration in Rural Oaxaca, Mexico: Dependency, Development, and the Household."

69. Cohen, *The Culture of Migration in Southern Mexico.*

70. Passel and Cohn, *Mexican Immigrants.*

71. Yoshikawa, Suárez-Orozco, and Gonzales, "Unauthorized Status and Youth Development in the United States."

72. The majority of Solagueño immigrants, male and female, work as dry cleaners. Some Solagueño immigrants work as janitors and some Solagueñas work as housekeepers or nannies.

73. Michael Kearney's "Transnational Oaxacan Indigenous Identity: The Case of Mixtecs and Zapotecs" and Lynn Stephen's *Transborder Lives: Indigenous Oaxacans in Mexico, California, and Oregon*; Leo Chavez's *Shadowed Lives: Undocumented Immigrants in American Society* and Seth Holmes's *Fresh Fruit, Broken Bodies: Migrant Farmworkers in the United States*; Fox and Rivera-Salgado, *Indigenous Mexican Migrants in the United States.*

74. Fox and Rivera-Salgado, *Indigenous Mexican Migrants in the United States*; Cruz-Manjarrez, *Zapotecs on the Move.*

75. Holmes, *Fresh Fruit, Broken Bodies.*

76. Blackwell, Boj Lopez, and Urrieta, "Critical Latinx Indigeneities"; Speed, "States of Violence: Indigenous Women Migrants in the Era of Neoliberal Multicriminalism."

77. Heidbrink, *Migranthood.*

78. Speed, *Incarcerated Stories*; Speed, "States of Violence: Indigenous Women Migrants in the Era of Neoliberal Multicriminalism."

79. Boj Lopez, "Discovering Dominga: Indigenous Migration and the Logics of Indigenous Displacement."

80. brown, *Pleasure Activism,* 13. Angeliza Sanchez, then an undergraduate at the University of California, Santa Barbara, first introduced me to the concept of pleasure activism through a grant for her research on Zapotec wedding practices from San Bartolomé Quialana. Leisy Abrego has also pointed to the connections between my conceptualization of *el goce comunal* and pleasure activism.

81. Gil, "Mujeres indígenas, fiesta y participación política."

82. Friedlander, "The Secularization of the Cargo System"; Kummels, *Indigeneity in Real Time.*

83. Gil, "Mujeres indígenas, fiesta y participación política"; Ramos Morales, "La propiedad comunal y el acceso a los recursos naturales."

84. Johnson, *Spaces of Conflict, Sounds of Solidarity,* 1.

Chapter 1

1. The photographs and home videos our parents sent to their parents in Solaga allowed our grandparents to meet their grandchildren, allowing them to circumvent the U.S.-Mexico border, which prevented many of our parents from returning to their hometown with their U.S.-born or raised children.

2. Martínez Luna, *Comunalidad y desarrollo.*

3. Robles Hernández and Cardoso Jiménez, *Floriberto Díaz*; Martínez Luna, "Conocimiento y comunalidad"; Rendón Monzón, *La comunalidad*; Sánchez-Antonio, "Genealogía de la comunalidad indígena."

4. Ramos Morales, *La propiedad comunal y el acceso a los recursos naturales.*

5. Nicolas, "'Soy de Zoochina': Transborder *comunalidad*"; Sánchez, "Reaffirming Indigenous Identity."

6. Gudeman, "Saints, Symbols, and Ceremonies."

7. Gross, "Religion and Respeto"; Marroquín, *El conflicto religioso Oaxaca, 1976–1992*; Ricard, *The Spiritual Conquest of Mexico*; Speed, *Incarcerated Stories.*

8. Arias, "La fiesta patronal en transformación."

9. Chance, *Conquest of the Sierra,* 166.

10. Nash, "Political Relations in Guatemala"; Wolf, *Sons of the Shaking Earth.*

11. Gross, "Religion and Respeto"; Whitecotton, *The Zapotecs.*

12. Whitecotton, *The Zapotecs.*

13. Chance, *Conquest of the Sierra.*

14. Chance, *Conquest of the Sierra.*

15. Chance, *Conquest of the Sierra*, 169.

16. Chance, *Conquest of the Sierra*, 133, emphasis in the original.

17. Chance, *Conquest of the Sierra*.

18. Cancian, *Economics and Prestige in a Maya Community*; Chance and Taylor, "Cofradías and Cargos"; Wolf, "Closed Corporate Peasant Communities in Mesoamerica and Central Java," *Sons of the Shaking Earth*.

19. Wolf, "Closed Corporate Peasant Communities in Mesoamerica and Central Java."

20. Wolf, "Closed Corporate Peasant Communities in Mesoamerica and Central Java."

21. Beezley, Martin, and French, "Introduction"; Chance and Taylor, "Cofradías and Cargos"; Whitecotton, *The Zapotecs*.

22. Kearney, *The Winds of Ixtepeji*; Nash, "Political Relations in Guatemala"; Tax, *Penny Capitalism*; Wolf, *Sons of the Shaking Earth*.

23. Friedlander, "The Secularization of the Cargo System."

24. Ventura Luna, *The Migration Experience as It Relates to Cargo Participation in San Miguel Cuevas, Oaxaca*.

25. Friedlander, "The Secularization of the Cargo System."

26. Gross, "Religion and Respeto"; Kearney and Besserer, "Oaxacan Municipal Governance in Transnational Context"; VanWey et al., "Community Organization, Migration, and Remittances in Oaxaca."

27. Joo, "International Migration and the Use of Remittances in the Local Sociocultural Structure in Oaxaca, Mexico"; VanWey, Tucker, and McConnell, "Community Organization, Migration, and Remittances in Oaxaca."

28. Caballero and Ríos Morales, "Impacto de la migración trasnacional entre los ñuu savi (mixtecos) y los bene xhon (zapotecos de la Sierra Norte) de Oaxaca."

29. Whitecotton, *The Zapotecs*, 218.

30. Gross, "Religion and Respeto."

31. The concept of *comunalidad* emerged from their university training or time in Escuelas Normales Rurales, and their politicization in the student movement of 1968. The concept of *comunalidad* emerged from Indigenous struggles in the late 1970s against land dispossession and resource extraction and in defense of community autonomy and better living conditions. Aquino Moreschi also traces the origins of *comunalidad* to these scholars' engagement with liberation theology and critical anthropology (in Mexico). These schools of thought challenged the Mexican state's assimilationist policies toward Indigenous peoples and destigmatized Indigeneity for community members, including ideas that blamed poverty and poor education on Indigenous peoples themselves, rather than on the state/structural conditions that kept Indigenous peoples at the margins of Mexican society. Social movements in Mexico and in Oaxaca have continually strengthened

and amplified the calls for Indigenous autonomy and the empowerment of Indigenous communities through their culture, helped destigmatize Indigeneity and empower community members to use their community knowledges, and conceptualized their way of knowing and being in the world according to their worldview. Indeed, in his theorization of *comunalidad*, Aquino Moreschi argues, Floriberto Díaz does not view Indigenous societies as opposite to or opposing the West, but as different from Western societies. In doing this, Díaz challenges the socially constructed distinction between Indigenous peoples and Spaniards. Aquino Moreschi, "La generación de la 'emergencia indígena' y el comunalismo oaxaqueño," "La comunalidad como epistemología del Sur."

32. Martínez Luna, *Comunalidad y desarrollo*.

33. Robles Hernández and Cardoso Jiménez, *Floriberto Díaz, Escrito. Comunalidad, energía viva del pensamiento mixe*.

34. Sánchez López, "Learning from the *paisanos*," 245. Emphasis added.

35. Robles Hernández and Cardoso Jiménez, *Floriberto Díaz*; Martínez Luna, "Conocimiento y comunalidad"; Rendón Monzón, *La comunalidad*; Sánchez-Antonio, "Genealogía de la comunalidad indígena."

36. Martínez Luna, *Comunalidad y desarrollo*.

37. Kearney, *The Winds of Ixtepeji*; Nash, "Political Relations in Guatemala"; Tax, *Penny Capitalism*; Wolf, *Sons of the Shaking Earth*.

38. The *cargo* system can also be understood as a hierarchical institution as it contains more "prestigious" roles at its higher ranks; however, officeholders must first give service to the community through lower-ranking *cargos*.

39. Martínez Luna, *Comunalidad y desarrollo*.

40. Korsbaek, "El comunalismo: Cambio de paradigma en la antropología mexicana a raíz de la globalización."

41. Aquino Moreschi, "La comunalidad como epistemología del Sur."

42. Aquino Moreschi, "La comunalidad como epistemología del Sur."

43. Nicolas, "'Soy de Zoochina': Transborder *comunalidad*."

44. Robles Hernández and Cardoso Jiménez, *Floriberto Díaz*; Martínez Luna, "Conocimiento y comunalidad."

45. The *cargo* system is associated with communal authority as general assemblies nominate or designate individuals to positions in the *cargo* system. While holding *cargo* office may no longer be plausible for Zoochinenses and other Serranos in diaspora, they continue to partake in practices of *comunalidad* both in their hometown and outside of their hometown. I suggest that these practices include participation in hometown festivities.

46. Those that would like to, or *gusten*, to be *mayordomos* may choose to sponsor items or events for the *fiesta*, such as the prize for a sporting event or covering the fees for a musical act.

47. Martínez Luna, "Conocimiento y comunalidad"; Mendoza Zuany, "Indigenousness without Ethnicity in the Sierra Norte of Oaxaca, Mexico."

48. The *comisión de festejos* begins meeting two months prior to patron saint celebrations to calculate the cost of that year's festivities. Donations collected from townspeople and remittances from hometown organizations in Oaxaca City, Mexico City, and Los Angeles, California, are used to buy food items and to book *cumbia, conjuntos,* or *norteño* bands and other entertainment during the festivities.

49. Cohen, *Cooperation and Community*; Magazine, "We All Put on the Fiesta Together."

50. Brandes, "Cargos Versus Cost"; Magazine, "We All Put on the Fiesta Together."

51. Cruz-Manjarrez, *Zapotecs on the Move.*

52. These practices are what I term *convivencia,* which I discuss further in Chapter 3.

53. Martínez Luna, "Conocimiento y comunalidad."

54. Martínez Luna, "Conocimiento y comunalidad."

55. Caballero and Ríos Morales, "Impacto de la migración trasnacional entre los ñuu savi (mixtecos) y los bene xhon (zapotecos de la Sierra Norte) de Oaxaca."

56. Caballero and Ríos Morales, "Impacto de la migración trasnacional entre los ñuu savi (mixtecos) y los bene xhon (zapotecos de la Sierra Norte) de Oaxaca," 180.

57. Emphasis added.

58. De Genova, "The Legal Production of Mexican/Migrant 'Illegality'"; Inda, *Targeting Immigrants.*

59. Martínez Luna, "Conocimiento y comunalidad."

60. Cohen, "Transnational Migration in Rural Oaxaca, Mexico"; Stephen, *Zapotec Women.*

61. Cohen, "Transnational Migration in Rural Oaxaca, Mexico."

62. Joo, "International Migration and the Use of Remittances in the Local Sociocultural Structure in Oaxaca, Mexico."

63. Joo, "International Migration and the Use of Remittances in the Local Sociocultural Structure in Oaxaca, Mexico," 30.

64. The dues paid to Solagueño hometown associations became an important source of money to build infrastructure in Solaga, ranging from the restoration of the municipal palace and community church to subsidizing aspects of annual patron saint celebrations in the community.

65. Nicolas, "'Soy de Zoochina': Transborder *comunalidad*," 53.

66. Sanchez, "Racial and Structural Discrimination toward the Children of Indigenous Mexican Immigrants."

67. One of my First Communion portraits is a picture taken at the party held in honor of me receiving this Catholic sacrament superimposed with a picture of my maternal grandparents taken in their home in Solaga, which makes it appear that we are in the same place.

68. My grandmother's back is turned to the camera so I cannot read her expression. The *Din Cansec* I knew, like her daughters and eldest granddaughter, loved to dance so I gather she too was enjoying the *jarabe*.

69. In the middle of the state of communal enjoyment.

70. I do not mean to dismiss the suffering in my grandfather or other Indigenous peoples' lives or to romanticize *el goce*. My grandfather lost his mother as a 3-year-old child and died in a tragic car accident in his 50s. His participation in and the satisfaction he drew from his contributions to communal life is what I and other Solagueños remember. In his short life, he experienced the joy of being in his *pueblo* with his *pueblo* countless times. His children, grandchildren, and great-grandchildren are still able to relish the *convivencia* and the goodwill he fostered through his communal involvement. I refuse to reduce my grandfather's life to the tragedies he experienced; instead I focus on the memories of the joy he experienced and allowed for us to experience.

71. Mendoza Zuany, "Indigenousness without Ethnicity in the Sierra Norte of Oaxaca, Mexico."

72. Maldonado Alvarado, *Autonomía y comunalidad India*.

Chapter 2

1. Some informants described themselves, community members, or objects and practices with Solagueño origin as "Solagan." This identifier seems to be an Anglicized version of "Solagueño" and a more localized version of "Oaxacan."

2. Matias's use of "cousins" refers to the reality that most second-generation Solagueños are biological kin. While I cannot trace our shared ancestor, I know Matias and I are blood relatives.

3. Blackwell, "Geographies of Indigeneity"; Magaña, "Multimodal Archives of Transborder Belonging."

4. Nájera and Maldonado, "Transnational Settler Colonial Formations and Global Capital."

5. Aquino Moreschi, "Las lógicas del no-reconocimiento y la lucha cotidiana de las migrantes zapotecas en Estados Unidos"; Aquino Moreschi, "La generación de la 'emergencia indígena' y el comunalismo oaxaqueño."

6. Batz, "Maya Cultural Resistance in Los Angeles"; Magaña, "Multimodal Archives of Transborder Belonging."

7. It is important to note that this citizenship is settler-created, as are the criteria through which one can be or become a citizen.

8. Chavez, *The Latino Threat*, 4.

9. Blackwell, "Líderes campesinas"; Blackwell, Boj Lopez, and Urrieta, "Critical Latinx Indigeneities."

10. Calderón, "Uncovering Settler Grammars in Curriculum," 315.

11. Alberto, "Coming Out as Indian"; Blackwell, Boj Lopez, and Urrieta, "Critical Latinx Indigeneities"; Calderón, "Uncovering Settler Grammars in Curriculum"; Razack, *Race, Space, and the Law*.

12. Calderón, "Uncovering Settler Grammars in Curriculum"; O'Brien, *Firsting and Lasting*. This national mythology has repercussions for the U.S.-born Latinxs and Mexicans, whose claims to citizenship are continuously questioned because of their racial background.

13. Alberto, "Coming Out as Indian."

14. Nájera and Maldonado, "Transnational Settler Colonial Formations and Global Capital." Drawing on Fujikane and Okamura (*Asian Settler Colonialism*), Blackwell, Boj Lopez, and Urrieta state that while Indigenous immigrants can be considered settlers, they do not all "have the political capacity to colonize Northern Native nations" ("Critical Latinx Indigeneities," 127).

15. Lytle Hernández, *City of Inmates*.

16. Lytle Hernández, *City of Inmates*.

17. Sepulveda, "Our Sacred Waters."

18. Lytle Hernández, *City of Inmates*.

19. Lytle Hernández, *City of Inmates*.

20. Vigil, *From Indians to Chicanos*; Wilson, "Cultural Politics of Race and Ethnicity."

21. Lytle Hernández, *City of Inmates*.

22. While Native encounters with missionaries ranged from more humane conversion efforts to brutal massacres, students learn sanitized versions of California missions and the Spanish priests who oversaw them. Spanish missionaries have become celebrated figures and are often treated as the predecessors of modern-day Latinxs (Urrieta and Calderón, "Critical Latinx Indigeneities"). This collapsing of history both ahistoricizes these figures and erases the racial hierarchies that informed their efforts to assimilate Native peoples and dispossess them of their lands.

23. Torres-Rouff, *Before LA*, 39.

24. Lytle Hernández, *City of Inmates*.

25. Torres-Rouff, *Before LA*, 39.

26. Torres-Rouff, *Before LA*.

27. Torres-Rouff, *Before LA*, 59.

28. Lytle Hernández, *City of Inmates*.

29. Chavez, *The Latino Threat*.

30. Torres-Rouff, *Before LA*.

31. Pulido, "Rethinking Environmental Racism."

32. Pulido, Barraclough, and Cheng, *A People's Guide to Los Angeles*.

33. Johnson, *Spaces of Conflict, Sounds of Solidarity*, 161.

34. Johnson, *Spaces of Conflict, Sounds of Solidarity*; Magaña, "Multimodal Archives of Transborder Belonging."

35. Pulido, "Rethinking Environmental Racism," 31.

36. Logan, Zhang, and Alba, "Immigrant Enclaves and Ethnic Communities in New York and Los Angeles"; Pulido, "Rethinking Environmental Racism."

37. Portes and Rumbaut, *Immigrant America*.

38. Johnson, *Spaces of Conflict, Sounds of Solidarity*; Magaña, "Multimodal Archives of Transborder Belonging." Latinx and Black Angelenos have become the latest targets of technologies of containment used against the Tongva, Mexican Californios, and other marginalized groups deemed unworthy of living in Los Angeles.

39. Pulido, "Rethinking Environmental Racism," 25.

40. Johnson, *Spaces of Conflict, Sounds of Solidarity*; Magaña, "Multimodal Archives of Transborder Belonging," 944; Pulido, "Rethinking Environmental Racism."

41. Navarro, "The South Central Los Angeles Eruption," 75.

42. Kim, Levin, and Botchwey, "Planning with Unauthorized Immigrant Communities."

43. Today, Mid-City and Koreatown are experiencing rapid gentrification.

44. Abrego and Gonzales, "Blocked Paths, Uncertain Futures."

45. Magaña, "Multimodal Archives of Transborder Belonging."

46. Pulido, "Rethinking Environmental Racism"; Torres-Rouff, *Before LA*.

47. Howell and Griffiths, *Gangs in America's Communities*.

48. Abrego and Gonzales, "Blocked Paths, Uncertain Futures"; Portes and Rumbaut, *Immigrant America*.

49. Chavez, *The Latino Threat*.

50. Rumbaut and Komaie, "Immigration and Adult Transitions."

51. Coutin, *Exiled Home*.

52. "Yeah, only Oaxacans. Only Oaxacan Koreans." LA Times Staff, "Inside the Room."

53. Portes and Rumbaut, *Immigrant America*; Zamora, *Racial Baggage*.

54. Boj Lopez, "Mobile Archives of Indigeneity"; Kearney, "Transnational Oaxacan Indigenous Identity"; Stephen, *Transborder Lives*.

55. Calderón, "Uncovering Settler Grammars in Curriculum," 315, 321; O'Brien, *Firsting and Lasting*.

56. Lytle Hernández, *City of Inmates*.

57. Lytle Hernández, *City of Inmates*; Torres-Rouff, *Before LA.*

58. Gutiérrez and Almaguer, "Introduction."

59. Chavez, *The Latino Threat*, 31.

60. Chavez, *The Latino Threat.*

61. Chavez, "Outside the Imagined Community."

62. Erikson, *Identity, Youth and Crisis.*

63. Chavez, *The Latino Threat*; Gonzales and Chavez, "Awakening to a Nightmare."

64. Gonzales, "Learning to Be Illegal"; Gonzales and Chavez, "Awakening to a Nightmare."

65. Coutin, *Exiled Home.*

66. Glenn, "Settler Colonialism as Structure."

67. Barillas-Chón, "Oaxaqueño/a Students' (Un)Welcoming High School Experiences"; Ruiz and Barajas, "Multiple Perspectives on the Schooling of Mexican Indigenous Students in the US"; Urrieta, "Las identidades también lloran/Identities Also Cry."

68. Nicolas, "Reclamando lo que es nuestro."

69. Chavez, *The Latino Threat*; Zamora, *Racial Baggage.*

70. Blackwell, Boj Lopez, and Urrieta, "Critical Latinx Indigeneities."

71. Flores Dorantes and Ruiz Torres, "Las Bandas de Viento."

72. Flores Dorantes and Ruiz Torres, "Las Bandas de Viento"; Muñoz, "Etnicidad y música"; Saldaña Ramirez, "Bandas de viento y sentido de comunidad entre los mixtecos en Morelos."

73. Sanchez, "Racial and Structural Discrimination toward the Children of Indigenous Mexican Immigrants."

74. Blackwell, "Geographies of Indigeneity," 164.

75. Kelley, *Race Rebels*; Johnson, *Spaces of Conflict, Sounds of Solidarity.*

76. Caballero and Ríos Morales, "Impacto de la migración trasnacional entre los ñuu savi (mixtecos) y los bene xhon (zapotecos de la Sierra Norte) de Oaxaca."

77. López Oro, "Black Caribs/Garifuna: Maroon Geographies of Indigenous Blackness."

78. Alberto, "Coming Out as Indian: On Being an Indigenous Latina in the US."

Chapter 3

1. Gross, "Religion and Respeto." This orientation toward a particular community of origin and its people has been described as *pueblismo* (Hirabayashi, *Cultural Capital*).

2. Indigenous and non-Indigenous scholars have written about the importance of *convivencia* to Indigenous communities. They have described *convivencia*

as "coexistence through sharing," "living together," and "sharing and being with others" (Gross, "Religion and Respeto"; Trinidad Galván, *Women Who Stay Behind*; Vasquez, "Mobile Postcards").

3. Heidbrink, *Migranthood*; Speed, *Incarcerated Stories*.

4. Vasquez Ruiz, "Mobile Postcards."

5. Asad and Hwang, "Indigenous Places and the Making of Undocumented Status in Mexico-US Migration"; De Genova, "The Legal Production of Mexican/Migrant 'Illegality.'"

6. The Immigration Reform and Control Act of 1986 allowed for the legalization of an estimated two million unauthorized immigrants who had been in the United States for at least five years (DeSipio and de la Garza, *U.S. Immigration in the Twenty-First Century: Making Americans, Remaking America*).

7. Stephen, *Transborder Lives*.

8. Emphasis added.

9. Menjívar and Abrego, "Legal Violence," 1386.

10. Enriquez, "Multigenerational Punishment"; García, *Living Juana Crow*.

11. Chavez, *The Latino Threat*.

12. While childhood may be conceptualized as "a time of only play and learning, or as a time without responsibilities" (Taft, *The Kids Are in Charge*, 3), Indigenous children engage in care work from an early age. Andean children in Peru, for example, may be relocated to a new household to accompany a lonely adult and help with household tasks (Leinaweaver, "On Moving Children," "Outsourcing Care: How Peruvian Migrants Meet Transnational Family Obligations"). Indigenous Guatemalan youth migrate transnationally as a collective and historically rooted survival strategy against racism, historical violence, and intergenerational structural inequality in Guatemala (Heidbrink, *Migranthood*). Indigenous youths' early experiences establish cultural norms and social expectations of kinship obligations and belonging that they maintain across generations and geography (Heidbrink, *Migranthood*). While migration may make them physically absent from their home communities, however, they continue to engage in carework and "shape household bonds and mediate conflict by providing emotional and social support to family members adapting to new cultural, social, and kinship networks in which they are embedded" (Heidbrink, *Migranthood*, 35).

13. Simpson, "The Ruse of Consent and the Anatomy of 'Refusal,'" 19.

14. Settler attempts to control Indigenous peoples' movement in the Los Angeles area can be traced to vagrancy laws created to incarcerate California's original Indigenous peoples who were then forced to build the historic pueblo of Los Angeles (Lytle Hernández, *City of Inmates*). Berg's ethnography about Andean Peruvians' migration demonstrates how race- and class-based ideas about Indigenous peoples as unfit for citizenship continue to permeate the lives of Indigenous

Peruvians and limit their opportunities for state-authorized international migration (Berg, *Mobile Selves*).

15. Clarsen, "Special Section on Settler-Colonial Mobilities," 42.

16. Blackwell, Boj Lopez, and Urrieta, "Critical Latinx Indigeneities."

17. The Fourteenth Amendment to the American constitution made U.S. citizenship accessible to Native Americans and formerly enslaved Blacks and their descendants, as well as the children of non-White immigrants, including the children of Indigenous Latinx immigrants (Chavez, *Anchor Babies and the Challenge of Birthright Citizenship*).

18. Sergio Martínez and Urrieta, "El carguero transnacional."

19. Urrieta and Martínez, "Diasporic Community Knowledge and School Absenteeism."

20. Sergio Martínez and Urrieta, "El carguero transnacional."

21. These staples include coffee, beans, and sugar cane. Coffee, in particular, is sent to relatives or sold by some Solagueños for consumption in the United States.

22. Magaña, *Cartographies of Youth Resistance;* Speed, *Incarcerated Stories.*

23. While patron saint celebrations are opportunities for *convivencia* in Indigenous communities in Mexico, the importance of *convivencia* is such that communities hold *convivios* exclusive to community members. In Solaga, these smaller gatherings occur at the end of patron saint festivities. While Solagueños have already spent several days celebrating their patron saint, patron saint celebrations consist of simultaneously occurring events in different parts of town and draw people from the surrounding communities. *Convivios* allow Solagueños to be in community with each other. These small-scale celebrations establish community membership and give community members the opportunity to interact with each other by dancing, eating, and chatting. Patron saint celebrations officially end with the *convivios* and signal that normal life will resume for Solagueño locals and members of the diaspora who will soon depart for their place of residence. In Los Angeles, *Solaga USA*, the Solagueño youth brass band, also holds *convivios*. These *convivios* are usually limited to band members and their parents. While band members and their parents spend a considerable amount of time together at practice, fundraisers, and performances, these small gatherings allow them to connect with each other outside of these events—where they are usually too busy to *convivir* in the truest sense of the notion. They thus create time and space to be together in community.

24. Nájera and Ortiz, "Expressing Communality."

25. Alberto, "Mestizaje desde Abajo," 236.

26. Alberto, "Mestizaje desde Abajo," 245–246.

27. As a result of my growing up in diaspora, community members have often *convivido* more than I have with my living and deceased relatives in the hometown.

Through memories of their *convivencia,* I feel like I too have been able to *convivir* and know my ancestors.

28. Díaz, "Resiste la poscolonia."

29. Reyes Basurto, Martínez, and Campbell, "What Is Community?"

30. Ruiz and Barajas, "Multiple Perspectives on the Schooling of Mexican Indigenous Students in the US."

31. Felix likely knew I also spoke Zapotec. During her brief time in Los Angeles, my grandmother spoke Zapotec in and outside of our home—something that until then had not been done in our household. Her presence ensured that I learned Zapotec at an early age and that I did not attach stigma to speaking an Indigenous language that my parents learned as children. During my return trips to Solaga, she recounted family and community stories in our native language, which allowed me to gain an understanding of our world rooted in our language.

32. Vera-Rosas and Guerrero, "Immigrant Identity Is 'Twin Skin' to Linguistic Identity."

33. Gross, "Religion and Respeto."

34. Aquino Moreschi ("La comunalidad como epistemología del Sur: Aportes y retos") suggests that *comunalidad* allows people to organize, *convivir,* and achieve a shared goal. Importantly, *convivencia* allows people to build communal relations and create shared experiences while working toward a common goal. *Convivencia* as part of a shared project allows a project to become a communal endeavor, rather than a solitary one.

35. Portes and Rumbaut, *Immigrant America;* Rumbaut, Massey, and Bean, "Linguistic Life Expectancies."

36. Ruiz and Barajas, "Multiple Perspectives on the Schooling of Mexican Indigenous Students in the US."

37. Reyes Basurto, Hernández Martínez, and Campbell, "What Is Community?"

38. Menjívar, "Living in Two Worlds?"; Rumbaut, "Severed or Sustained Attachments?"

39. Stephen, *Transborder Lives,* 207.

40. Levitt, "Roots and Routes."

41. Nicolas, "'Soy de Zoochina': Transborder *comunalidad.*"

42. Xóchitl Chávez, "Oaxacan Indigenous Women Musicians' Collective Songwriting Process on the Title Track of Mujeres"; Nicolas, "'Soy de Zoochina': Transborder *comunalidad.*"

43. Stephen, *Transborder Lives,* 18.

44. Aquino-Moreschi and Contreras-Pastrana, "Comunidad, jóvenes y generación."

45. Wessendorf, "'Roots Migrants.'"

46. Aquino-Moreschi and Contreras-Pastrana, "Comunidad, jóvenes y generación."

47. Shkodriani and Gibbons, "Individualism and Collectivism among University Students in Mexico and the United States," 766.

48. Diaz-Loving and Draguns, "Culture, Meaning, and Personality in Mexico and in the United States."

49. Martínez Luna, *Comunalidad y desarrollo.*

50. Miranda, "'They were tough, those old women before us,'" 382.

51. Silko as quoted in Miranda, "'They were tough, those old women before us,'" 382.

52. In the communities Hilaria Cruz descends from, gossiping can be dangerous, with those being labeled as gossips or those divulging gossip being murdered. See Cruz, "Between Insiders and Outsiders."

53. Miranda, "'They were tough, those old women before us.'"

Chapter 4

1. Zapotec peoples often keep records of exchanges made through the *gozona* system, and community members can refer to it to fulfill their obigations through the system (Beals, "Gifting, Reciprocity, Savings, and Credit in Peasant Oaxaca").

2. Carlos's comments are reflective of the difficulties of living in mixed-status families, that is, a family composed of both documented and undocumented family members.

3. *Champurrado* is a chocolate-based drink that Solagueños prepare with water, *masa,* and *panela.* These food items and drinks are traditionally consumed during the main feast day of patron saint celebrations in Solaga.

4. In Chapter 1, I demonstrate how musical exchanges through the *gozona* system allow Solagueños to foster good relations between their community and neighboring communities. These relationships are important beyond the Sierra Norte itself, especially as Serranos continue to rely on these networks in diaspora.

5. In Solagueño Zapotec (*dixa xhon*), musicians are referred to as *bene wekuell.* Since music is central to Solagueño community life, *bi wekuell* in Solaga and in the diaspora are key figures at Solagueño events. While community events are open to all, Solagueño youth band members and their parents are more likely to be present at community events, providing them with a unique appreciation of the aural. Solagueños who are not in the town's bands, however, also cooperate in staging community events, whether by showing their support by purchasing food during *kermeses* or donating items for patron saint celebrations.

6. The *cargo* system is an Indigenous institution that organizes social, political, and ritual life and defines membership in the community. Through a system of rotating positions, or *cargos,* men provide service to the community throughout

their adult life beginning as policemen and working their way up to the most prestigious position of president of the municipality. Ríos Morales argues that from a young age children construct their social world around the religious and civil expectations that are placed on them. Fulfilling these responsibilities allows them to establish and solidify themselves as members of the community. See Ríos Morales, "Béne wha lhall, béne lo ya'a."

7. Rosado-May et al., "Innovation as a Key Feature of Indigenous Ways of Learning"; Urrieta, "Learning by Observing and Pitching In and the Connections to Native and Indigenous Knowledge Systems."

8. Samuels et al. define soundscape as "a publicly circulating entity that is a produced effect of social practices, politics, and ideologies while also being implicated in the shaping of those practices, politics, and ideologies" ("Soundscapes," 330). Alex Chávez (*Sounds of Crossing*) challenges the notion of soundscape in its theorization of sound as geographically bounded. Instead, he turns to the body to show how aural poetics physically and emotionally move and connect people and places across space and time. Both Chávez and Carlos, the emcee mentioned in the text, recognize the importance of musicians to the movement of sound.

9. Blackwell, "Geographies of Indigeneity."

10. Aquino Moreschi, "Las lógicas del no-reconocimiento y la lucha cotidiana de las migrantes zapotecas en Estados Unidos"; Aquino Moreschi, "La generación de la 'emergencia indígena' y el comunalismo oaxaqueño"; Aquino Moreschi, "La comunalidad como epistemología del Sur"; Martínez Luna, *Eso que llaman comunalidad*; Mendoza Zuany, "Indigenousness without Ethnicity in the Sierra Norte of Oaxaca, Mexico."

11. Aurality "encompass[es] immediate and mediated practices of listening that construct perceptions and understandings of nature, bodies, voices, and technologies in particular moments and places" (Minks and Gautier, "Music, Language, Aurality," 25).

12. Minks and Gautier, "Music, Language, Aurality."

13. Caballero and Ríos Morales, "Impacto de la migración trasnacional entre los ñuu savi (mixtecos) y los bene xhon (zapotecos de la Sierra Norte) de Oaxaca."

14. Smith, "Beyond Geography's Visible Worlds," 524.

15. Johnson, *Spaces of Conflict, Sounds of Solidarity*, 1–2.

16. Martínez Luna (*Comunalidad y desarrollo*) suggests that resistance is fundamental to Indigenous identities and is embedded in various aspects of quotidian life, including music, work, and *fiestas*. Porras-Kim, "Whistling and Language Transfiguration."

17. Blackwell, Boj Lopez, and Urrieta, "Critical Latinx Indigeneities"; Boj Lopez, "Mobile Archives of Indigeneity"; Speed, "States of Violence."

18. While in his statement he says Oaxaca, which could be interpreted as Oaxaca City or places in the state of Oaxaca, his reference to the basketball courts is a direct reference to Solaga since most events for the patron saint celebration take place on or around the basketball court in the center of town.

19. Solagueños across generations and across borders build and maintain relations with other Serrano *paisanos*, people from surrounding communities in the Sierra Juarez. Local and diasporic Serrano visitors are familiar with the *fiesta* based on their own community's cultural practices and are attuned to the communal meaning behind these practices. They are also able to tap into preexisting ancestral and personal relationships they have with Solaga and with Solagueños.

20. Urrieta and Martínez, "Diasporic Community Knowledge and School Absenteeism."

21. For Matias, a dystopic world is a world where neither Oaxaca nor its cultures are known. This is in direct contrast to Matias's and other Los Angeles–based Oaxacan youths' reality, in which by merely mentioning their parents' home state, some teachers recognize they are likely to have a musical background. An outsider's recognition of Oaxacan culture instills youth like Matias with a sense of pride. This pride makes a difference to Oaxacan youth who may face discrimination because of their ethnic background.

22. Aquino Moreschi, "Las lógicas del no-reconocimiento y la lucha cotidiana de las migrantes zapotecas en Estados Unidos"; Aquino Moreschi, "La generación de la 'emergencia indígena' y el comunalismo oaxaqueño"; Martínez Luna, *Eso que llaman comunalidad*.

23. Klaver, *From the Land of the Sun to the City of Angels*.

24. Nicolas, "Soy de Zoochina: Zapotecs across Generations."

25. Matias is trained as a jazz musician, for example, and indicated that he and other Oaxacan jazz musicians incorporate aspects of jazz into Oaxacan music.

26. My godfather was born to Solagueño immigrants in Mexico City. He and his siblings traveled to Solaga for patron saint celebrations during summer vacations. As a teenager, he migrated to Los Angeles, where he met and married a U.S.-born Solagueña. Thus, while he was born in diaspora, my *padrino* is also enmeshed in Solagueño soundscapes.

27. Porras-Kim, "Whistling and Language Transfiguration."

28. Porras-Kim, "Whistling and Language Transfiguration," 234.

29. Robinson writes that "settler colonial forms of perception, or 'tin ears,' ... disallow us from understanding Indigenous song as both an aesthetic thing and as more-than-song" (Robinson, *Hungry Listening*, 45).

30. Robinson, *Hungry Listening*.

31. A *tlayuda* is a dish that consists of a thin, toasted tortilla topped with lard, a bean paste, *quesillo*, cabbage, and pork or beef.

32. Caballero and Ríos Morales, "Impacto de la migración trasnacional entre los ñuu savi (mixtecos) y los bene xhon (zapotecos de la Sierra Norte) de Oaxaca."

33. Corona and Madrid, "Introduction," 5. Similarly, Stó:lō scholar Dylan Robinson emphasizes "how critical listening positionality emerges through an intersection of sqwálewel (thinking-feeling) between two Indigenous forms of attentiveness, one that is brought from 'home' ... the other from the lands on which [we are guests]" (Robinson, *Hungry Listening*, 51).

34. Urrieta, "Familia and comunidad-based saberes."

35. Blackwell, "Geographies of Indigeneity." Shannon Speed (*Incarcerated Stories*) urges scholars to acknowledge that present-day power relations are not a result of the colonial past but are part of an ongoing settler colonial process. In so doing, we destabilize the notion that settlers are "from here" and acknowledge that Indigenous people in North America and Latin America live in a state of ongoing occupation.

36. Ramón Martínez and Mesinas, "Linguistic Motherwork in the Zapotec Diaspora"; Speed, *Incarcerated Stories*.

37. Speed, *Incarcerated Stories*.

38. Lomnitz, "Bordering on Anthropology."

39. Urrieta, "Learning by Observing and Pitching In and the Connections to Native and Indigenous Knowledge Systems."

40. The accounts Díaz gathered include testimonies of abuse ranging from children having to haul a bucket of water for each Zapotec word they spoke to being whipped on their hands with cables or poles by schoolteachers. See Díaz, "Resiste la poscolonia. "

41. Despite the establishment of bilingual (Spanish and Zapotec) schools in Solaga, children and youth are more fluent in Spanish than in Zapotec. This may be a result of the goal of these schools being to teach Indigenous children the national language and curriculum (Urrieta, "Learning by Observing and Pitching In and the Connections to Native and Indigenous Knowledge Systems") without addressing the linguistic ideologies embedded in these practices.

42. Ruiz and Barajas, "Multiple Perspectives on the Schooling of Mexican Indigenous Students in the US."

43. Barillas-Chón, "Oaxaqueño/a Students' (Un)Welcoming High School Experiences"; Morales, Saravia, and Pérez-Iribe, "Multilingual Mexican-Origin Students' Perspectives on Their Indigenous Heritage Language"; Perez, Vasquez, and Buriel, "Zapotec, Mixtec, and Purepecha Youth"; Urrieta and Calderón, "Challenging Critical Latinx Indigeneities."

44. Urrieta and Calderón, "Challenging Critical Latinx Indigeneities."

45. Blackwell, Boj Lopez, and Urrieta, "Critical Latinx Indigeneities"; Speed, *Incarcerated Stories*; Urrieta, Mesinas, and Martínez, "Critical Latinx Indigeneities and Education."

46. Urrieta and Calderón, "Challenging Critical Latinx Indigeneities."

47. Morales, Saravia, and Pérez-Iribe, "Multilingual Mexican-Origin Students' Perspectives on Their Indigenous Heritage Language."

48. Morales, Saravia, and Pérez-Iribe, "Multilingual Mexican-Origin Students' Perspectives on Their Indigenous Heritage Language," 116.

49. Morales, Saravia, and Pérez-Iribe, "Multilingual Mexican-Origin Students' Perspectives on Their Indigenous Heritage Language"; Perez, Vasquez, and Buriel, "Zapotec, Mixtec, and Purepecha Youth."

50. Morales, Saravia, and Pérez-Iribe, "Multilingual Mexican-Origin Students' Perspectives on Their Indigenous Heritage Language"; Perez, Vasquez, and Buriel, "Zapotec, Mixtec, and Purepecha Youth."

51. One can easily access Marcial's music on YouTube and Facebook, but recordings of these performances do not resonate as much as when these songs are performed live whether by Marcial or other community members. While Solagueños at this event pulled out their cellphones to record Bartolome, they were equally as interested in capturing the Solagueño youth band, *bi wekuell* born in diaspora who through their aural practices enable the performance of Marcial's songs.

52. Ramón Martínez and Mesinas, "Linguistic Motherwork in the Zapotec Diaspora."

53. Muehlmann, "Spread your ass cheeks"; Nicolas, "Soy de Zoochina: Zapotecs across Generations"; Urrieta, "Identity, Violence, and Authenticity."

54. Turino, *Music as Social Life*.

55. Language serves and has served as a marker of Indigeneity in official state records (Morales, Saravia, and Pérez-Iribe, "Multilingual Mexican-Origin Students' Perspectives on Their Indigenous Heritage Language"; Muehlmann, "Spread your ass cheeks").

56. Language and music are part of a semiotic field of meaning that Serranos engage with. Faudree suggests that "viewing music and language as part of a full semiotic field will further ongoing conversations about how to decenter texts as a core unit of analysis, while providing the tools for examining them holistically and assessing their relative importance (and unimportance) by positioning texts alongside other collections of signs, sonic and otherwise" ("Music, Language, and Texts," 520).

57. Faudree, "Music, Language, and Texts," 250.

58. Robinson, *Hungry Listening*, 38.

59. Robinson, *Hungry Listening*.

60. Alex Chávez, *Sounds of Crossing*.

61. Madrid, *Nor-tec rifa!*

62. Membership in Indigenous Oaxacan communities is not a birthright; community members must fulfill their obligations to their community through the

cargo system or through participating in other key aspects of community life, like playing in the local brass band (Denicourt, "Así nos tocó vivir").

63. Payan Ramirez, "Prácticas comunales en la escoleta de La Banda de Viento de Tamazulápam del Espíritu Santo Mixe, Oaxaca."

64. Sánchez-López, "Learning from the *paisanos*."

65. This socialization may include participating in the *cargo* system once they reach adolescence or running small errands (like dropping off tortillas at *la casa de la comisión* for visitors) during patron saint celebrations.

66. Maldonado Alvarado, *Autonomía y comunalidad India*; Ríos Morales, "Béne wha lhall, béne lo ya'a."

67. Mesinas and Perez, "Cultural Involvement, Indigenous Identity, and Language."

68. Battiste, *Indigenous Knowledge and Pedagogy in First Nations Education*; Rosado-May et al., "Innovation as a Key Feature of Indigenous Ways of Learning"; Urrieta, "Learning by Observing and Pitching In and the Connections to Native and Indigenous Knowledge Systems."

69. Urrieta, "Learning by Observing and Pitching In and the Connections to Native and Indigenous Knowledge Systems," 369.

70. Rosado-May et al., "Innovation as a Key Feature of Indigenous Ways of Learning."

71. Mendoza Zuany, "Indigenousness without Ethnicity in the Sierra Norte of Oaxaca, Mexico."

72. Maldonado Alvarado, *Autonomía y comunalidad India*.

73. Nicolas, "Soy de Zoochina: Zapotecs across Generations"; Nicolas, "'Soy de Zoochina': Transborder *comunalidad*."

74. Martínez Luna, "Conocimiento y comunalidad"; Mendoza Zuany, "Indigenousness without Ethnicity in the Sierra Norte of Oaxaca, Mexico."

75. Aquino Moreschi, "La comunalidad como epistemología del Sur"; Maldonado Alvarado, *Autonomía y comunalidad India*.

Conclusion

1. Flores-Marcial, "A History of Guelaguetza in Zapotec Communities of the Central Valleys of Oaxaca, 16th Century to the Present."

2. When did you arrive from your ... *pueblo*? Or how do you say it?

3. "Yes. *Pueblo*. You call it a *pueblo*."

4. Adding *-ucho* or *-ito* to *pueblo* would add a pejorative connotation to the word.

5. In this context, "el gabacho" refers to the United States but it can also refer to a White, American male.

6. I later asked one of the cousins that was with me how he felt about the inter-action. He responded, "Se olló un poco discriminatorio, ¿no?" ("It sounded a bit

discriminatory, right?"). Moments later he shared his experience on a trip he took with a Oaxacan politician to Baja California, where the local government signed an agreement with Oaxacan authorities that local officials would not discriminate against Oaxacan migrants because of their Indigenous background. "That topic would be great for your research," my cousin added.

7. "They're ugly!"; LA Times Staff, "Inside the Room."

8. Kauanui, "A Structure, Not an Event."

9. Morgan, *Ancient Society*.

10. O'Brien, *Firsting and Lasting*.

11. TallBear, "Genomic Articulations of Indigeneity"; TallBear, *Native American DNA*.

12. Hooker, *Theorizing Race in the Americas*.

13. Vasconcelos as quoted in Hooker, *Theorizing Race in the Americas*, 155.

14. Hernández Castillo, *Histories and Stories from Chiapas*; Wade, *Race and Ethnicity in Latin America*.

15. Figueroa-Vásquez, *Decolonizing Diasporas*, 10.

16. Friedlander, *Being Indian in Hueyapan*; Kearney, "Transnational Oaxacan Indigenous Identity"; Wilson, "Cultural Politics of Race and Ethnicity."

17. Sue, *Land of the Cosmic Race*.

18. Díaz, "Resiste la poscolonia."

19. Ruiz and Barajas, "Multiple Perspectives on the Schooling of Mexican Indigenous Students in the US."

20. Sánchez-López, "Learning from the *paisanos*."

REFERENCES

Abrego, Leisy J., and Roberto G. Gonzales. "Blocked Paths, Uncertain Futures: The Postsecondary Education and Labor Market Prospects of Undocumented Latino Youth." *Journal of Education for Students Placed at Risk* 15, no. 1–2 (2010): 144–157.

Aikau, Hokulani K. "Indigeneity in the Diaspora: The Case of Native Hawaiians at Iosepa, Utah." *American Quarterly* 62, no. 3 (2010): 477–500.

Alberto, Lourdes. "Coming Out as Indian: On Being an Indigenous Latina in the US." *Latino Studies* 15, no. 2 (2017): 247–253.

Alberto, Lourdes. "Mestizaje desde Abajo: Zapotec Visual Cultures and Decolonial Mestizaje in the Photography of Citlali Fabián." *Aztlan: A Journal of Chicano Studies* 46, no. 2 (2021): 235–250.

Anzaldúa, Gloria. *Making Face, Making Soul/Haciendo Caras: Creative and Critical Perspectives by Feminists of Color.* San Francisco: Aunt Lute Books, 1990.

Aquino Moreschi, Alejandra. "La comunalidad como epistemología del Sur: Aportes y retos." *Cuadernos del Sur, Revista de Ciencias Sociales* (2013): 7–19.

Aquino Moreschi, Alejandra. "La generación de la 'emergencia indígena' y el comunalismo oaxaqueño: Genealogía de un proceso de descolonización." *Cuadernos del Sur, Revista de Ciencias Sociales* 15, no. 29 (2010): 7–21.

Aquino Moreschi, Alejandra. "Las lógicas del no-reconocimiento y la lucha cotidiana de las migrantes zapotecas en Estados Unidos: Breve etnografía del servicio doméstico." *Cuicuilco* 17, no. 49 (2010): 221–242.

Aquino-Moreschi, Alejandra, and Isis Contreras-Pastrana. "Comunidad, jóvenes y generación: Disputando subjetividades en la Sierra Norte de Oaxaca." *Revista Latinoamericana de Ciencias Sociales, Niñez y Juventud* 14, no. 1 (2016): 463–475.

Archuleta, Elizabeth. "'I Give You Back': Indigenous Women Writing to Survive." *Studies in American Indian Literatures* 18, no. 4 (2006): 88–114.

Arias, Patricia. "La fiesta patronal en transformación: Significados y tensiones en las regiones migratorias." *Migración y desarrollo* 9, no. 16 (2011): 147–180.

Asad, Asad L., and Jackelyn Hwang. "Indigenous Places and the Making of Undocumented Status in Mexico-US Migration." *International Migration Review* 53, no. 4 (2019): 1032–1077.

Barillas-Chón, David W. "Oaxaqueño/a Students' (Un)Welcoming High School Experiences." *Journal of Latinos and Education* 9, no. 4 (2010): 303–320.

Battiste, Marie. *Indigenous Knowledge and Pedagogy in First Nations Education.* National Working Group on Education and the Minister of Indian Affairs. Indian and Northern Affairs Canada (INAC), Ottawa, Ontario, October 2002. https://www.nipissingu.ca/sites/default/files/2018-06/Indigenous%20Knowledge%20and%20Pedagogy%20.pdf.

Batz, Giovanni. "Maya Cultural Resistance in Los Angeles: The Recovery of Identity and Culture among Maya Youth." *Latin American Perspectives* 41, no. 3 (2014): 194–207.

Beals, Ralph L. "Gifting, Reciprocity, Savings, and Credit in Peasant Oaxaca." *Southwestern Journal of Anthropology* 26, no. 3 (1970): 231–241.

Beezley, William H., Cheryl E. Martin, and William E. French. "Introduction: Constructing Consent, Inciting Conflict." *In Rituals of Rule, Rituals of Resistance: Public Celebrations and Popular Culture in Mexico,* edited by William H. Beezley, Cheryl E. Martin, and William E. French, xiii–xxxii. Lanham, MD: Rowman & Littlefield, 1994.

Berg, Ulla D. *Mobile Selves: Race, Migration, and Belonging in Peru and the US.* New York: NYU Press, 2017.

Blackwell, Maylei. "Geographies of Indigeneity: Indigenous Migrant Women's Organizing and Translocal Politics of Place." *Latino Studies* 15, no. 2 (2017): 156–181.

Blackwell, Maylei. "Líderes campesinas: Nepantla Strategies and Grassroots Organizing at the Intersection of Gender and Globalization." *Aztlán: A Journal of Chicano Studies* 35, no. 1 (2010): 13–47.

Blackwell, Maylei, Floridalma Boj Lopez, and Luis Urrieta. "Critical Latinx Indigeneities." *Latino Studies* 15, no. 2 (2017): 126–137.

Boj Lopez, Floridalma. "Discovering Dominga: Indigenous Migration and the Logics of Indigenous Displacement." *Kalfou* 7, no. 2 (2020): 392–407.

Boj Lopez, Floridalma. "Mobile Archives of Indigeneity: Building La Comunidad Ixim through Organizing in the Maya Diaspora." *Latino Studies* 15 (2017): 201–218.

Brandes, Stanley. "Cargos Versus Cost: Sharing in Mesoamerican Fiestas, with Special Reference to Tzintzuntzan." *Journal of Anthropological Research* 37, no. 3 (1981): 209–225.

brown, adrienne maree. *Pleasure Activism: The Politics of Feeling Good.* Chico, CA: AK Press, 2019.

Caballero, Juan Julián, and Manuel Ríos Morales. "Impacto de la migración trasnacional entre los ñuu savi (mixtecos) y los bene xhon (zapotecos de la Sierra Norte) de Oaxaca." *Coordinación de humanidades* (2004): 137.

Calderón, Dolores. "Uncovering Settler Grammars in Curriculum." *Educational Studies* 50, no. 4 (2014): 313–338.

Cancian, Frank. *Economics and Prestige in a Maya Community: The Religious Cargo System in Zinacantan.* Redwood City, CA: Stanford University Press, 1965.

Cardoso, Lawrence A. *Mexican Emigration to the United States 1897–1931.* Tucson: University of Arizona Press, 1980.

Casillas, Dolores Inés. *Sounds of Belonging: US Spanish-Language Radio and Public Advocacy.* New York: NYU Press, 2014.

Celis, et al. *San Andrés Solaga, Lugar de hojas regadas: breve esbozo de historia local.* Oaxaca, México: Colegio Superior para la Educación Integral Intercultural de Oaxaca, 2009.

Chance, John K. *Conquest of the Sierra: Spaniards and Indians in Colonial Oaxaca.* Norman: University of Oklahoma Press, 1989.

Chance, John K., and William B. Taylor. "Cofradías and Cargos: An Historical Perspective on the Mesoamerican Civil-Religious Hierarchy." *American Ethnologist* 12, no. 1 (1985): 1–26.

Chávez, Alex E. *Sounds of Crossing: Music, Migration, and the Aural Poetics of Huapango Arribeño.* Durham, NC: Duke University Press, 2017.

Chavez, Leo R. *Anchor Babies and the Challenge of Birthright Citizenship.* Redwood City, CA: Stanford University Press, 2020.

Chavez, Leo R. *Covering Immigration: Popular Images and the Politics of the Nation.* Berkeley: University of California Press, 2001.

Chavez, Leo R. *The Latino Threat: Constructing Immigrants, Citizens, and the Nation.* Redwood City, CA: Stanford University Press, 2013.

Chavez, Leo R. "Outside the Imagined Community: Undocumented Settlers and Experiences of Incorporation." *American Ethnologist* 18, no. 2 (1991): 257–278.

Chavez, Leo R. *Shadowed Lives: Undocumented Immigrants in American Society.* Fort Worth, TX: Harcourt Brace College, 1998.

Chávez, Xóchitl C. "Oaxacan Indigenous Women Musicians' Collective Songwriting Process on the Title Track of Mujeres." *Americas (Lincoln, Neb.)* 29 (2020): 121–133.

Clarsen, Georgine. "Introduction: Special Section on Settler-Colonial Mobilities." *Transfers* 5, no. 3 (2015): 41–48.

Clifford, James. "Diasporas." *Cultural Anthropology* 9, no. 3 (1994): 302–338.

Cohen, Jeffrey H. *Cooperation and Community: Society and Economy in Oaxaca.* Austin: University of Texas Press, 1999.

Cohen, Jeffrey. *The Culture of Migration in Southern Mexico.* Austin: University of Texas Press, 2004.

Cohen, Jeffrey H. "Transnational Migration in Rural Oaxaca, Mexico: Dependency, Development, and the Household." *American Anthropologist* 103, no. 4 (Dec. 2001): 954–967.

Corona, Ignacio, and Alejandro L. Madrid. "Introduction: The Postnational Turn in Music Scholarship and Music Marketing." In *Postnational Musical Identities: Cultural Production, Distribution, and Consumption in a Globalized Scenario,* edited by Ignacio Corona and Alejandro L. Madrid, 3–22. Lanham, MD: Lexington Books, 2008.

Coutin, Susan Bibler. *Exiled Home: Salvadoran Transnational Youth in the Aftermath of Violence.* Durham, NC: Duke University Press, 2016.

Cruz, Hilaria. "Between Insiders and Outsiders: When an Indigenous Researcher Conducts Studies in Her Own Community." *Language Documentation & Conservation* 23 (2021): 43–63.

Cruz-Manjarrez, Adriana. *Zapotecs on the Move: Cultural, Social, and Political Processes in Transnational Perspective.* New Brunswick, NJ: Rutgers University Press, 2013.

De Genova, Nicholas. "The Legal Production of Mexican/Migrant 'Illegality.'" *Latino Studies* 2, no. 2 (2004): 160–185.

Denicourt, Jérémie. "'Así nos tocó vivir': Práctica de la comunidad y territorios de reciprocidad en la Sierra Mixe de Oaxaca." *Trace (México, DF)* 65 (2014): 23–36.

DeSipio, Louis, and de la Garza, Rodolfo O. *U.S. Immigration in the Twenty-First Century: Making Americans, Remaking America.* Boulder, CO: Westview Press, 2015.

Díaz, Tercero. "Resiste la poscolonia: Un retrato de las lenguas maternas en Mexico." Centro Nacional de Comunicacion Social, 2018.

Diaz-Loving, Rolando, and Juris G. Draguns. "Culture, Meaning, and Personality in Mexico and in the United States." In *Personality and Person Perception across Cultures,* edited by Yueh-Ting Lee, Clark R. McCauley, and Juris G. Draguns, 103–126. Mahwah, NJ: Lawrence Erlbaum, 1999.

Enriquez, Laura E. "Multigenerational Punishment: Shared Experiences of Undocumented Immigration Status within Mixed-Status Families." *Journal of Marriage and Family* 77, no. 4 (2015): 939–953.

Erikson, Erik H. *Identity, Youth and Crisis.* New York: W. W. Norton, 1968.

Faudree, Paja. "Music, Language, and Texts: Sound and Semiotic Ethnography." *Annual Review of Anthropology* 41 (2012): 519–536.

Figueroa-Vásquez, Yomaira C. *Decolonizing Diasporas: Radical Mappings of Afro-Atlantic Literature.* Evanston, IL: Northwestern University Press, 2020.

Fitzpatrick, Peter. "'We know what it is when you do not ask us': Nationalism as Racism." In *Nationalism, Racism and the Rule of Law*, edited by Peter Fitzpatrick, 3–26. Hanover, NH: Dartmouth University Press, 1995.

Flores Dorantes, Felipe, and R. A. Ruiz Torres. "Las Bandas de Viento: Una rica y ancestral tradición de Oaxaca." In *Bandas de viento en México*, edited by Georgina Flores Mercado, 183–205. Instituto Nacional de Antropología e Historia, 2015.

Flores-Marcial, Xochitl Marina. "A History of Guelaguetza in Zapotec Communities of the Central Valleys of Oaxaca, 16th Century to the Present." PhD diss., University of California, Los Angeles, 2015.

Fox, Jonathan, and Gaspar Rivera-Salgado. "Building Civil Society among Indigenous Migrants." In *Indigenous Mexican Migrants in the United States*, edited by Jonathan Fox and Gaspar Rivera-Salgado, 1–68. La Jolla, CA: Center for US-Mexican Studies, 2004.

Friedlander, Judith. *Being Indian in Hueyapan*, rev. ed. London: Macmillan, 2006.

Friedlander, Judith. "The Secularization of the Cargo System: An Example from Postrevolutionary Central Mexico." *Latin American Research Review* 16, no. 2 (1981): 132–143.

Fujikane, Candace, and Jonathan Y. Okamura. *Asian Settler Colonialism: From Local Governance to the Habits of Everyday Life in Hawaii?* Honolulu: University of Hawaii Press, 2008.

Gamio, Manuel. *Forjando Patria: Pro-Nacionalismo*. Ann Arbor: University of Michigan Library, 1916.

García, San Juanita. "*Living Juana Crow*: The Spillover Consequences of Living a Deportation Threat on Mexican-Origin Women's Mental Health." Unpublished manuscript, 2021.

Garroutte, Eva Marie. *Real Indians: Identity and the Survival of Native America.* Berkeley: University of California Press, 2003.

Gaudry, Adam. "Communing with the Dead: The "New Métis," Métis Identity Appropriation, and the Displacement of Living Métis Culture." *American Indian Quarterly* 42, no. 2 (2018): 162–190.

Gegeo, David Welchman. "Cultural Rupture and Indigeneity: The Challenge of (Re)visioning 'Place' in the Pacific." *Contemporary Pacific: A Journal of Island Affairs* 13, no. 2 (2001): 491–507.

Gil, Yásnaya Elena A. "Mujeres indígenas, fiesta y participación política." *Dossier, consultado mayo* 12 (2020).

Glenn, Evelyn Nakano. "Settler Colonialism as Structure: A Framework for Comparative Studies of US Race and Gender Formation." *Sociology of Race and Ethnicity* 1, no. 1 (2015): 52–72.

Gonzales, Roberto G. "Learning to Be Illegal: Undocumented Youth and Shifting Legal Contexts in the Transition to Adulthood." *American Sociological Review* 76, no. 4 (2011): 602–619.

Gonzales, Roberto G., and Leo R. Chavez. "'Awakening to a Nightmare': Abjectivity and Illegality in the Lives of Undocumented 1.5-generation Latino Immigrants in the United States." *Current Anthropology* 53, no. 3 (2012): 255–281.

Gross, Toomas. "Religion and Respeto: The Role and Value of Respect in Social Relations in Rural Oaxaca." *Studies in World Christianity* 21, no. 2 (2015): 119–139.

Grossman, Jonathan. "Toward a Definition of Diaspora." *Ethnic and Racial Studies* 42, no. 8 (2019): 1263–1282.

Gudeman, Stephen. "Saints, Symbols, and Ceremonies." *American Ethnologist* 3, no. 4 (1976): 709–729.

Gutiérrez, Kris D., and Barbara Rogoff. "Cultural Ways of Learning." In *Knowledge, Values and Educational Policy*, edited by Harry Daniels, Hugh Lauder, and Jill Porter, 114–125. New York: Routledge, 2012.

Gutiérrez, Ramón, and Tomás Almaguer. "Introduction." In *The New Latino Studies Reader: A Twenty-First-Century Perspective*, edited by Ramón A. Gutiérrez and Tomás Almaguer, 1–18. University of California Press, 2016.

Heidbrink, Lauren. *Migranthood: Youth in a New Era of Deportation*. Redwood City, CA: Stanford University Press, 2020.

Hernández Castillo, Aída R. *Histories and Stories from Chiapas: Border Identities in Southern Mexico*. Austin: University of Texas Press, 2001.

Hirabayashi, Lane Ryo. *Cultural Capital: Mountain Zapotec Migrant Associations in Mexico City*. Tucson: University of Arizona Press, 1993.

Holmes, Seth. *Fresh Fruit, Broken Bodies: Migrant Farmworkers in the United States*. Berkeley: University of California Press, 2013.

Hooker, Juliet. *Theorizing Race in the Americas: Douglass, Sarmiento, Du Bois, and Vasconcelos*. New York: Oxford University Press, 2019.

Howell, James C., and Elizabeth Griffiths. *Gangs in America's Communities*. Thousand Oaks, CA: Sage, 2018.

Huang, Wei-Jue, William C. Norman, Gregory P. Ramshaw, and William J. Haller. "Transnational Leisure Experience of Second-Generation Immigrants: The Case of Chinese-Americans." *Journal of Leisure Research* 47, no. 1 (2015): 102–124.

Hurtado, Aída. *Intersectional Chicana Feminisms: Sitios y Lenguas*. Tucson: University of Arizona Press, 2020.

Inda, Jonathan Xavier. *Targeting Immigrants: Government, Technology, and Ethics*. Maiden, MA: Blackwell, 2006.

Johnson, Gaye Theresa. *Spaces of Conflict, Sounds of Solidarity*. Berkeley: University of California Press, 2013.

Joo, Jong-Taick. "International Migration and the Use of Remittances in the Local Sociocultural Structure in Oaxaca, Mexico." (2012).

Kauanui, J. Kēhaulani. "'A Structure, Not an Event': Settler Colonialism and Enduring Indigeneity." *Emergent Critical Analytics for Alternative Humanities* 5, no. 1 (2016). https://doi.org/10.25158/L5.1.7.

Kearney, Michael. "Transnational Oaxacan Indigenous Identity: The Case of Mixtecs and Zapotecs." *Identities Global Studies in Culture and Power* 7, no. 2 (2000): 173–195.

Kearney, Michael. *The Winds of Ixtepeji: World View and Society in a Zapotec Town.* Long Grove, IL: Waveland Press, 1972.

Kearney, Michael, and Federico Besserer. "Oaxacan Municipal Governance in Transnational Context." In *Indigenous Mexican Migrants in the United States,* edited by Jonathan Fox and Gaspar Rivera-Salgado, 449–468. La Jolla, CA: Center for US-Mexican Studies, 2004.

Kelley, Robin D. G. *Race Rebels: Culture, Politics, and the Black Working Class.* New York: Free Press, 1994.

Kim, Anna J., Josh M. Levin, and Nisha D. Botchwey. "Planning with Unauthorized Immigrant Communities: What Can Cities Do?" *Journal of Planning Literature* 33, no. 1 (2018): 3–16.

Klaver, Jeanine F. I. *From the Land of the Sun to the City of Angels: The Migration Process of Zapotec Indians from Oaxaca, Mexico to Los Angeles.* Netherlands Geographical Society, 1997.

Kresge, Lisa. "Indigenous Oaxacan Communities in California: An Overview." *California Institute for Rural Studies* (2007).

Korsbaek, Leif. "El comunalismo: Cambio de paradigma en la antropología mexicana a raíz de la globalización." *Argumentos (México, DF)* 22, no. 59 (2009): 101–123.

Kummels, Ingrid. *Indigeneity in Real Time: The Digital Making of Oaxacalifornia.* New Brunswick, NJ: Rutgers University Press, 2023.

LA Times Staff. "Inside the Room: The Entire LA City Council Racist Audio Leak, Annotated by our Experts." *LA Times,* November 21, 2022. https://www.latimes.com/california/story/2022-11-2la-city-council-racist-audio-leak-transcription- annotation.

Leinaweaver, Jessaca B. "On Moving Children: The Social Implications of Andean Child Circulation." *American Ethnologist* 34, no. 1 (2007): 163–180.

Leinaweaver, Jessaca B. "Outsourcing Care: How Peruvian Migrants Meet Transnational Family Obligations." *Latin American Perspectives* 37, no. 5 (2010): 67–87.

Levitt, Peggy. "Roots and Routes: Understanding the Lives of the Second Generation Transnationally." *Journal of Ethnic and Migration Studies* 35, no. 7 (2009): 1225–1242.

Logan, John R., Wenquan Zhang, and Richard D. Alba. "Immigrant Enclaves and Ethnic Communities in New York and Los Angeles." *American Sociological Review* 67, no. 2 (2002): 299–322.

Lomnitz, Claudio. "Bordering on Anthropology: The Dialectics of a National Tradition in Mexico." *Revue de synthèse* 121, no. 3–4 (2000): 345–379.

López Oro, Paul Joseph. "Black Caribs/Garifuna: Maroon Geographies of Indigenous Blackness." *Small Axe: A Caribbean Journal of Criticism* 25, no. 3 (2021): 134–146.

Loza, Mireya. *Defiant Braceros: How Migrant Workers Fought for Racial, Sexual, and Political Freedom*. Chapel Hill, NC: UNC Press Books, 2016.

Lytle Hernández, Kelly. *City of Inmates: Conquest, Rebellion, and the Rise of Human Caging in Los Angeles, 1771–1965*. Chapel Hill: UNC Press Books, 2017.

Madrid, Alejandro L. *Nor-tec rifa!: Electronic Dance Music from Tijuana to the World*. New York: Oxford University Press, 2008.

Magaña, Maurice Rafael. *Cartographies of Youth Resistance: Hip-Hop, Punk, and Urban Autonomy in Mexico*. Berkeley: University of California Press, 2020.

Magaña, Maurice Rafael. "Multimodal Archives of Transborder Belonging: Murals, Social Media, and Racialized Geographies in Los Angeles." *American Anthropologist* 124, no. 4 (2022): 703–720.

Magazine, Roger. "'We All Put on the Fiesta Together': Interdependence and the Production of Active Subjectivity through Cargos in a Highland Mexican Village." *Journal of Latin American and Caribbean Anthropology* 16, no. 2 (2011): 296–314.

Maldonado Alvarado, Benjamín. *Autonomía y comunalidad India. Enfoques y propuestas desde Oaxaca*. México, Centro INAH Oaxaca, Secretaría de Asuntos Indígenas, Coalición de Maestros y Promo-tores Indígenas de Oaxaca, A.C., Centro de Encuentros y Diálogos Interculturales, 2002.

Marroquín, Enrique. *El conflicto religioso Oaxaca, 1976–1992*. Mexico: UNAM, 2007.

Martínez, Ramón Antonio, and Melisa Mesinas. "Linguistic Motherwork in the Zapotec Diaspora: Zapoteca Mothers' Perspectives on Indigenous Language Maintenance." *Association of Mexican American Educators Journal* 13, no. 2 (2019): 122–144.

Martínez, Sergio M., and Luis Urrieta Jr. "El carguero transnacional: Continuidad cultural de una comunidad michoacana." *Estudios sociales (Hermosillo, Son.)* 17, no. 33 (2009): 111–134.

Martínez Luna, Jaime. *Comunalidad y desarrollo: Culturas populares e indígenas*. Gobierno del estado de Oaxaca, 2004.

Martínez Luna, Jaime. "Conocimiento y comunalidad." *Bajo el Volcán* 15, no. 23 (2015): 99–12.

Martínez Luna, Jaime. *Eso que llaman comunalidad*. Consejo Nacional para la Cultura y las Artes, Secretaria de Cultura del Gobierno del Estado de Oaxaca, Colección Diálogos, 2010.

Massey, Douglas S., Rafael Alarcón, Jorge Durand, and Humberto González. *Return to Aztlan: The Social Process of International Migration from Western Mexico*. Berkeley: University of California Press, 1990.

Massey, Douglas S., Jorge Durand, and Nolan J. Malone. *Beyond Smoke and Mirrors: Mexican Immigration in the Area of Economic Integration*. New York: Russell Sage Foundation, 2003.

Mendoza Zuany, Rosa Guadalupe. "Indigenousness without Ethnicity in the Sierra Norte of Oaxaca, Mexico: Natives, Outsiders and Community-Based Identities." *Antipoda. Revista de Antropología y Arqueología* 19 (2014): 45–68.

Menjívar, Cecilia. "Living in Two Worlds? Guatemalan-origin Children in the United States and Emerging Transnationalism." *Journal of Ethnic and Migration Studies* 28, no. 3 (2002): 531–552.

Menjívar, Cecilia, and Leisy Abrego. "Legal Violence: Immigration Law and the Lives of Central American Immigrants." *American Journal of Sociology* 117, no. 5 (2012): 1380–1421.

Mesinas, Melissa, and William Perez. "Cultural Involvement, Indigenous Identity, and Language: An Exploratory Study of Zapotec Adolescents and Their Parents." *Hispanic Journal of Behavioral Sciences* 38, no. 4 (2016): 482–506.

Minks, Amanda, and Ana María Ochoa Gautier. "Music, Language, Aurality: Latin American and Caribbean Resoundings." *Annual Review of Anthropology* 50 (2021): 23–39.

Miranda, Deborah A. "'They were tough, those old women before us': The Power of Gossip in Isabel Meadows's Narratives." *Biography* 39, no. 3 (2016): 373–401.

Morales, P. Zitlali, Lydia A. Saravia, and María Fernanda Pérez-Iribe. "Multilingual Mexican-Origin Students' Perspectives on Their Indigenous Heritage Language." *Association of Mexican American Educators Journal* 13, no. 2 (2019): 91–121.

Morgan, Lewis Henry. *Ancient Society*. Tucson: University of Arizona Press, 1985.

Muehlmann, Shaylih. "'Spread your ass cheeks': And Other Things that Should Not Be Said in Indigenous Languages." *American Ethnologist* 35, no. 1 (2008): 34–48.

Muñoz, Alfonso. "Etnicidad y música: Estudio de caso de una comunidad zapoteca de emigrantes en la ciudad de México." Bachelor's thesis, Escuela Nacional de Antropología e Historia, 1994.

Nájera, Lourdes Gutiérrez, and Korinta Maldonado. "Transnational Settler Colonial Formations and Global Capital." *American Quarterly* 69, no. 4 (2017): 809–821.

Nájera, Lourdes Gutiérrez, and Ana D. Alonso Ortiz. "Expressing Communality: Zapotec Death and Mourning across Transnational Frontiers." In *Transnational*

Death, edited by Samira Saramo, Eerika Koskinen-Koivisto, and Hanna Snellman, 85–99. Helsinki: Studia Fennica Ethnologica, 2019.

Nash, Manning. "Political Relations in Guatemala." *Social and Economic Studies* 7, no. 1 (1958): 65–75. http://www.jstor.org/stable/27851138.

Navarro, Armando. "The South Central Los Angeles Eruption: A Latino Perspective." *Amerasia Journal* 19, no. 2 (1993): 69–86.

Nicolas, Brenda. "Reclamando lo que es nuestro: Identity Formation among Zapoteco Youth in Oaxaca and Los Angeles." M.A. thesis, University of California, San Diego, 2012.

Nicolas, Brenda. "'Soy de Zoochina': Transborder *comunalidad* Practices among Adult Children of Indigenous Migrants." *Latino Studies* 19, no. 1 (2021): 47–69.

Nicolas, Brenda. "Soy de Zoochina: Zapotecs across Generations in Diaspora Re-creating Identity and Sense of Belonging." Ph.D. diss., UCLA, 2017.

O'Brien, Jean M. *Firsting and Lasting: Writing Indians Out of Existence in New England*. Minneapolis: University of Minnesota Press, 2010.

Ortiz, Laura Velasco, and Dolores París Pombo. "Indigenous Migration in Mexico and Central America Interethnic Relations and Identity Transformations." *Latin American Perspectives* 41, no. 3 (2014): 5–25.

Ortiz Elizondo, Hector, and Rosalva Aida Hernández Castillo. "Constitutional Amendments and New Imaginings of the Nation: Legal Anthropological and Gendered Perspectives on 'Multicultural' Mexico." *PoLAR: Political and Legal Anthropology Review* 19, no. 1 (1996): 59–66.

Passel, Jeffrey S., and D. D'Vera Cohn. *Mexican Immigrants: How Many Come? How Many Leave?* Washington, D.C.: Pew Hispanic Center, 2009.

Payan Ramirez, Mercedes Alejandra. "Prácticas comunales en la escoleta de La Banda de Viento de Tamazulápam del Espíritu Santo Mixe, Oaxaca." M.A. thesis, Universidad Nacional Autónoma de México, 2017.

Perez, William, Rafael Vasquez, and Raymond Buriel. "Zapotec, Mixtec, and Purepecha Youth." In *Raciolinguistics: How Language Shapes Our Ideas about Race*, edited by H. Samy Alim, John R. Rickford, and Arnetha F. Ball, 255–272. New York: Oxford University Press, 2016.

Porras-Kim, Gala. "Whistling and Language Transfiguration: Zapotec Tones as Contemporary Art and Strategy for Resistance." *Hispanic American Historical Review* 96, no. 2 (2016): 233–237.

Portes, Alejandro, and Rubén G. Rumbaut. *Immigrant America: A Portrait*, 4th ed. Berkeley: University of California Press, 2014.

Pulido, Laura. "Rethinking Environmental Racism: White Privilege and Urban Development in Southern California." *Annals of the Association of American Geographers* 90, no. 1 (2000): 12–40.

Pulido, Laura, Laura Barraclough, and Wendy Cheng. *A People's Guide to Los Angeles*. Berkeley: University of California Press, 2012.

Ramos Morales, Mario Fernando. "La propiedad comunal y el acceso a los recursos naturales: El caso de los zapotecos de la Sierra Juárez de Oaxaca, México." Paper presented at the 10th Biennial Conference of the International Association for the Study of Common Property, Oaxaca, Mexico, August 2004. https://hdl.handle.net/10535/279.

Razack, Sherene, ed. *Race, Space, and the Law: Unmapping a White Settler Society*. Roseville, MN: Between the Lines, 2002.

Rendón Monzón, Juan José. *La comunalidad: Modo de vida en los pueblos indios*. México: Consejo Nacional para la Cultura y las Artes, 2004.

Reyes Basurto, Griselda, Carmen Hernández Martínez, and Eric W. Campbell. "What Is Community? Perspectives from the Mixtec Diaspora in California." In *Revitalizing Endangered Languages: A Practical Guide*, edited by Justyna Olko and Julia Sallabank, 100–102. New York: Cambridge University Press, 2021.

Ricard, Robert. *The Spiritual Conquest of Mexico: An Essay on the Apostolate and the Evangelizing Methods of the Mendicant Orders in New Spain, 1523–1572*. Berkeley: University of California Press, 1974.

Ríos Morales, Manuel de Jesús. "Béne wha lhall, béne lo ya'a: Identidad y etnicidad en la Sierra Norte Zapoteca de Oaxaca." PhD diss., Leiden University, 2011.

Rivera-Salgado, Gaspar. "Transnational Indigenous Communities: The Intellectual Legacy of Michael Kearney." *Latin American Perspectives* 41, no. 3 (2014): 26–46. https://doi.org/10.1177/0094582X13518753.

Robinson, Dylan. *Hungry Listening: Resonant Theory for Indigenous Sound Studies*. Minneapolis: University of Minnesota Press, 2020.

Robles Hernández, Sofía, and Rafael Cardoso Jiménez, eds. *Floriberto Díaz, Escrito: Comunalidad, energía viva del pensamiento mixe*. UNAM, 2007.

Rosado-May, Francisco J., Luis Urrieta Jr., Andrew Dayton, and Barbara Rogoff. "Innovation as a Key Feature of Indigenous Ways of Learning: Individuals and Communities Generating Knowledge." In *Handbook of the Cultural Foundations of Learning*, edited by Na'ilah Suad Nasir, Carol D. Lee, Roy Pea, and Maxine McKinney de Royston, 79–96. New York: Routledge, 2020.

Ruiz, Nadeen T., and Manuel Barajas. "Multiple Perspectives on the Schooling of Mexican Indigenous Students in the US: Issues for Future Research." *Bilingual Research Journal* 35, no. 2 (2012): 125–144.

Rumbaut, Rubén G. "Immigration, Incorporation, and Generational Cohorts in Historical Contexts." In *Historical Influences on Lives and Aging*, edited by K. Warner Schaie and Glen Elder, 43–88. New York: Springer, 2005.

Rumbaut, Rubén G. "Severed or Sustained Attachments? Language, Identity, and Imagined Communities in the Post-immigrant Generation." In *The Changing*

Face of Home: The Transnational Lives of the Second Generation, edited by Peggy Levitt and Mary C. Waters, 43–95. New York: Russell Sage Foundation, 2002.

Rumbaut, Rubén G., and Golnaz Komaie. "Immigration and Adult Transitions." *Future Child* 20, no. 1 (2010): 43–66.

Rumbaut, Rubén G., Douglas S. Massey, and Frank D. Bean. "Linguistic Life Expectancies: Immigrant Language Retention in Southern California." *Population and Development Review* 32, no. 3 (2006): 447–460.

Saldaña Ramirez, Adriana. "Bandas de viento y sentido de comunidad entre los mixtecos en Morelos." *Inventio* 13, no. 30 (2017): 23–29.

Saldívar, Emiko, and Casey Walsh. "Racial and Ethnic Identities in Mexican Statistics." *Journal of Iberian and Latin American Research* 20, no. 3 (2014): 455–475.

Samuels, David W., Louise Meintjes, Ana Maria Ochoa, and Thomas Porcello. "Soundscapes: Toward a Sounded Anthropology." *Annual Review of Anthropology* 39 (2010): 329–345.

Sanchez, Daina. "Racial and Structural Discrimination toward the Children of Indigenous Mexican Immigrants." *Race and Social Problems* 10, no. 4 (2018): 306–319.

Sánchez, Gabriela Kovats. "Reaffirming Indigenous Identity: Understanding Experiences of Stigmatization and Marginalization among Mexican Indigenous College Students." *Journal of Latinos and Education* 19, no. 1 (2018): 31–44.

Sánchez-Antonio, Juan Carlos. "Genealogía de la comunalidad indígena: Descolonialidad, transmodernidad y diálogos inter-civilizatorios." *Latin American Research Review* 56, no. 3 (2021): 696–710.

Sánchez-López, Luis. "Learning from the *paisanos*: Coming to Consciousness in Zapotec LA." *Latino Studies* 15, no. 2 (2017): 242–246.

Sepulveda, Charles. "Our Sacred Waters." *Decolonization: Indigeneity, Education & Society* 7, no. 1 (2018): 40–58.

Shkodriani, Gina M., and Judith L. Gibbons. "Individualism and Collectivism among University Students in Mexico and the United States." *Journal of Social Psychology* 135, no. 6 (1995): 765–772.

Simpson, Audra. *Mohawk Interruptus: Political Life across the Borders of Settler States*. Durham, NC: Duke University Press, 2014.

Simpson, Audra. "The Ruse of Consent and the Anatomy of 'Refusal': Cases from Indigenous North America and Australia." *Postcolonial Studies* 20, no. 1 (2017): 18–33.

Smith, Susan J. "Beyond Geography's Visible Worlds: A Cultural Politics of Music." *Progress in Human Geography* 21, no. 4 (1997): 502–529.

Smithers, Gregory D. "'What is an Indian?' The Enduring Question of American Indian Identity." In *Native Diasporas: Indigenous Identities and Settler*

Colonialism in the Americas, edited by Gregory D. Smithers and Brooke N. Newman, 1–27. Lincoln: University of Nebraska Press, 2014.

Speed, Shannon. "States of Violence: Indigenous Women Migrants in the Era of Neoliberal Multicriminalism." *Critique of Anthropology* 36, no. 3 (2016): 280–301.

Speed, Shannon. *Incarcerated Stories: Indigenous Women Migrants and Violence in the Settler-Capitalist State*. Chapel Hill: UNC Press Books, 2019.

Stephen, Lynn. "Indigenous Transborder Citizenship: FIOB Los Angeles and the Oaxaca Social Movement of 2006." *Latin American and Caribbean Ethnic Studies* 9, no. 2 (2014): 115–137.

Stephen, Lynn. *Transborder Lives: Indigenous Oaxacans in Mexico, California, and Oregon*. Durham, NC: Duke University Press, 2007.

Stephen, Lynn. *Zapotec Women*. Austin: University of Texas Press, 1991.

Sue, Christina. *Land of the Cosmic Race: Race Mixture, Racism, and Blackness in Mexico*. New York: Oxford University Press, 2013.

Taft, Jessica K. *The Kids Are in Charge: Activism and Power in Peru's Movement of Working Children*. New York: NYU Press, 2019.

TallBear, Kim. "Genomic Articulations of Indigeneity." *Social Studies of Science* 43, no. 4 (2013): 509–533. https://doi.org/10.1177/0306312713483893.

TallBear, Kim. *Native American DNA: Tribal Belonging and the False Promise of Genetic Science*. Minneapolis: Univesity of Minnesota Press.

Tax, Sol. *Penny Capitalism: A Guatemalan Indian Community*. Chicago: University of Chicago Press, 1963.

Torres-Rouff, David Samuel. *Before LA: Race, Space, and Municipal Power in Los Angeles, 1781–1894*. New Haven, CT: Yale University Press, 2013.

Trinidad Galván, Ruth. *Women Who Stay Behind: Pedagogies of Survival in Rural Transmigrant Mexico*. Tucson: University of Arizona Press, 2015.

Tsuda, Takeyuki. "Is Native Anthropology Really Possible?" *Anthropology Today* 31, no. 3 (2015): 14–17.

Tuhiwai Smith, Linda. "The Native and the Neoliberal Down Under: Neoliberalism and 'Endangered Authenticities.'" In *Indigenous Experience Today*, edited by Marisol de la Cadena and Orin Starn, 333–352. New York: Bloomsbury Academic, 2007.

Turino, Thomas. *Music as Social Life: The Politics of Participation*. Chicago: University of Chicago Press, 2008.

United States Census Bureau. *Los Angeles city, California*. Data.Census.Gov <https://www.census.gov/quickfacts/fact/table/losangelescitycalifornia/PST045222> (February 23, 2024).

Urrieta, Luis Jr. "Diasporic Community Smartness: Saberes (knowings) beyond Schooling and Borders." *Race Ethnicity and Education* 19, no. 6 (2016): 1186–1199.

Urrieta, Luis Jr. "Familia and comunidad-based saberes: Learning in an Indigenous Heritage Community." *Anthropology & Education Quarterly* 44, no. 3 (2013): 320–335.

Urrieta, Luis Jr. "Identity, Violence, and Authenticity: Challenging Static Conceptions of Indigeneity." *Latino Studies* 15, no. 2 (2017): 254–261.

Urrieta, Luis Jr. "Las identidades también lloran/Identities Also Cry: Exploring the Human Side of Latina/o Indigenous Identities." *Educational Studies* 34 (2003): 147–168.

Urrieta, Luis Jr. "Learning by Observing and Pitching In and the Connections to Native and Indigenous Knowledge Systems." *Advances in Child Development and Behavior* 49 (2015): 357–379.

Urrieta, Luis Jr., and Dolores Calderón. "Challenging Critical Latinx Indigeneities: Unpacking Indigeneity from Within and Outside of Latinized Entanglements." *Association of Mexican American Educators Journal* 13, no. 2 (2019): 145–174.

Urrieta, Luis Jr., and Sergio Martínez. "Diasporic Community Knowledge and School Absenteeism: Mexican Immigrant Pueblo Parents' and Grandparents' Postcolonial Ways of Educating." *Interventions* 13, no. 2 (2011): 256–277.

Urrieta, Luis Jr., Melissa Mesinas, and Ramón Antonio Martínez. "Critical Latinx Indigeneities and Education: An Introduction." *Association of Mexican American Educators Journal* 13, no. 2 (2019): 1–14.

VanWey, Leah Karin, Catherine M. Tucker, and Eileen Diaz McConnell. "Community Organization, Migration, and Remittances in Oaxaca." *Latin American Research Review* 40, no. 1 (2005): 83–107.

Vasquez Ruiz, Michelle. "Mobile Postcards: Zapotec Imagined Mobility." *Mobilities* 17, no. 2 (2022): 285–299.

Ventura Luna, Silvia. *The Migration Experience as It Relates to Cargo Participation in San Miguel Cuevas, Oaxaca.* 2010.

Vera-Rosas, Gretel H., and Perla M. Guerrero. "Immigrant Identity Is 'Twin Skin' to Linguistic Identity: Tracing the Afterlife of Deportation in Mexico City." *American Quarterly* 73, no. 3 (2021): 507–533.

Vigil, James Diego. *From Indians to Chicanos: The Dynamics of Mexican-American Culture.* Prospect Heights, IL: Waveland Press, 1998.

Wade, Peter. *Race and Ethnicity in Latin America.* Chicago: Pluto Press, 1997.

Wessendorf, Susanne. "'Roots Migrants': Transnationalism and 'Return' among Second-Generation Italians in Switzerland." *Journal of Ethnic and Migration Studies* 33, no. 7 (2007): 1083–1102.

Whitecotton, Joseph W. *The Zapotecs: Princes, Priests, and Peasants.* Norman: University of Oklahoma Press, 1977.

Wilson, Patrick C. "Cultural Politics of Race and Ethnicity." In *The Anthropology of Latin America and the Caribbean,* edited by Harry Sanabria, 110–145. New York: Routledge, 2007.

Wolf, Eric. "Closed Corporate Peasant Communities in Mesoamerica and Central Java." *Southwestern Journal of Anthropology* 13, no. 1 (1957): 1–18.

Wolf, Eric. *Sons of the Shaking Earth.* Chicago: University of Chicago Press, 1959.

Wolfe, Patrick. "Settler Colonialism and the Elimination of the Native." *Journal of Genocide Research* 8, no. 4 (2006): 387–410.

Yoshikawa, Hirokazu, Carola Suárez-Orozco, and Roberto G. Gonzales. "Unauthorized Status and Youth Development in the United States: Consensus Statement of the Society for Research on Adolescence." *Journal of Research on Adolescence* 27, no. 1 (2017): 4–19.

Zacarías, Plutarco Aquino. "Nuestra comunalidad: Reflexiones desde Yalalag." *Cuadernos del Sur: Revista de Ciencias Sociales* 34 (2013): 91–98.

Zamora, Sylvia. *Racial Baggage: Mexican Immigrants and Race across the Border.* Redwood City, CA: Stanford University Press, 2022.

INDEX

Printed in the USA
CPSIA information can be obtained
at www.ICGtesting.com
JSHW021102250924
70303JS00005B/6